sandra lee
Semi-Homemade® Desserts

miramax books

HYPERION

New York

sandra lee
Semi-Homemade® Desserts

Easy Delicious Desserts and Nothing Is Made from Scratch

COVER PHOTO: JOE BUISSINK

ISBN 1-4013-5927-2

First Paperback Edition
10 9 8 7 6 5 4 3 2 1

dedication and thank-you

DEDICATION

To my fellow Semi-Homemakers, may God bless you with every dream!

To the apples of my eye, Bruce, Aspen, and Sunny

To the sweetest things I've ever known, my nieces and nephews,
Scott, Danielle, Brandon, Austen, Stephanie, Bryce, and Blake

To my brothers and sisters, who are thoughtful, loving, supportive, and brilliant,
Cindy, Kim, Rich, John Paul, and Bobby
and
In memory of my Grandma Lorraine and my Aunt Betty,
for all the sundresses, sundaes, and celebrations.

All My Love—Always
s.l.

THANK YOU

To the Production Team

Hilary, Ed, Linda, Rochelle, Marykay, Denise, Pamela, Kathy, Ann, Brenda, Andy, John, Cindy, and Mark

To the Publishing Team

Jonathan, Kathy, Hilary, Kristin, Bruce, Jen, and the entire Miramax, Hyperion, Time Warner AOL teams

To the Business Team

Bert, Barry, Harvey, Bob, Lori, Steve, Charles, Eli, Barbara, Harold, Lee, Simon, Monique, Wendy, Mark, John, and Rob

To my team of "Girlfriends"

Mary, Colleen, Barbara, Marion, Jane, Julie, Vinny, Wendy, Fran, Arianna, Tina, Ghada, Lisa, and Danielle

I'm so incredibly lucky to have you all!

INTRODUCTION FROM MARY HART

The first thing I thought when I saw my friend Sandra Lee's cookbook was, "This food is absolutely gorgeous." The second thing I thought was, "These recipes are actually doable, even for someone with my crazy schedule!" Here, at last, was food we could all make and enjoy; recipes that make us want to rush right into the kitchen and start cooking, recipes that look as spectacular as they taste.

When Sandra told me her second cookbook was going to be a dessert book, I was thrilled. Sandra loves good food, but she's absolutely passionate about desserts. And I may be a fitness fanatic, but I can seldom pass up a chance to indulge my sweet tooth.

Semi-Homemade® Desserts is more than a collection of recipes; it's a way of life. Sandra loves sharing good food; she loves opening her home to others, making it a beautiful and inviting gathering place for family and friends. But, like so many of us, Sandra's life is busy and full, with much to do and little time to do it in. Her book is an endless stream of ideas, an abundance of simple, yet creative, recipes that are a breeze to make and a treat to serve. Sandra teaches us to have fun with dessert, to try something new, to pair the familiar with the unexpected. She shows us that it's not the grand gestures that impress, but the little touches—a sprinkle of sugared rose petals, a drizzle of warm honey, the cool elegance of fresh mint with lime.

And she does it all with such style. Sandra's desserts are as effervescent and fun to be around as she is. Every dessert is a centerpiece—beautifully prepared, imaginatively garnished and served on a simple white plate, with Sandra's signature touch of playfulness that says, "It is dessert, after all." Whether serving chocolate-covered cherries atop a shot of spiked syrup or tying a big white ribbon around The Perfect Package cake, Sandra knows that a dash of style is as important as a dollop of substance. Whatever the occasion—a bake sale at school, a romantic rendezvous, or a party with friends—you can flip open a Sandra Lee cookbook and know that anything you make will look as sensational as it tastes.

Dessert can be many things—a simple pleasure, a fun extravagance, a delicious way to treat yourself. But most of all, a dessert should be worth every bite. And, for that, Sandra Lee takes the cake.

Here's wishing you sweet success,

Mary Hart

Mary Hart

sugar

LETTER FROM SANDRA

We all want to have our cake and eat it too. Now, with *Semi-Homemade®*, you can have your cake, your cookies, your candies, your cobblers, even your kisses, and eat them, too!

In today's hectic world, with the constant crunch of jobs, families, and errands, it's all too easy to get caught up in the craziness and forget to savor the sweeter side of life. What better way to take a little time for ourselves than with a deliciously decadent dessert that lifts our spirits and makes our taste buds sing?

I've always had a sweet spot for dessert. Growing up, I spent many happy hours watching my grandma bake, helping her sift flour, measure sugars and spices, roll out doughs, and decorate each dessert to make it special. To her, and now to me, dessert is love—the delicious byproduct of caring hands and a happy heart. I enjoyed baking with my grandma so much I'd take the money I earned from berry picking or selling handmade crafts and buy the *Wilton®* books on cake decorating, adding to my collection whenever I could.

As the years went by and time became more precious, I'd search for shortcuts. How could I make each recipe more quickly, saving valuable time while preserving the even more valuable taste? The answer was to mix scratch ingredients with ready-made products from the grocery store, experimenting with the blend until I'd get it just right. I can now proudly say I get the same quality and flavor baking *Semi-Homemade®* as when I baked from scratch. Of course, the main ingredient in every recipe is still the same—love.

I personally love every single dessert in this book. Each one is unabashedly rich and unapologetically indulgent—a marvelous medley of flavors and textures that linger lovingly in your mouth. I never feel one bit of guilt. Dessert, like life, is short and sweet. I treasure every melt-in-your-mouth moment and hope you will, too.

This book is full of fast and fabulous treats created with a *Semi-Homemaker's* busy life in mind. It's created for you and dedicated to you. You'll find desserts for special days…and desserts that make any day special. You'll find desserts to give your family…and desserts to give as gifts. Desserts that satisfy your sweet tooth…and desserts that satisfy your soul.

Dessert is one of life's simple pleasures—especially when made with ease, the *Semi-Homemade®* way. We all need to take time to smell the roses, particularly when they're buttercream.

With a Big Chocolate Kiss,

Sandra Lee

tips

SHAVING

To shave chocolate into elegant curls, drag a sharp vegetable peeler down the side of a block of chocolate (or a chocolate bar), using one fluid motion. The chocolate should be at room temperature.

TRIMMING

If your oven isn't level or the temperature properly calibrated, cakes may come out uneven. Using a serrated knife, level your cakes by trimming any high spots or rough edges.

LAYERING

To divide a cake into layers, use a ruler to insert a row of toothpicks evenly around the cooled cake. Using the toothpicks as a guide, gently "saw" the cake horizontally with a sharp serrated knife.

CUTTING

For perfect slices, dip a chopping knife into hot water and dry it with a towel before every cut. A hot knife cuts more smoothly, and continual cleaning prevents bits of cake from clinging to the slices.

From the Package

HELPFUL HINTS, TIPS, AND TRICKS

Checking oven: Always preheat the oven 15 minutes before putting cakes in to bake. Buy a spring-action oven thermometer that clips onto your oven rack. An oven that is too hot or too cold can ruin baked goods. Put the rack in the middle of the oven, and the cakes in the center of the rack.

Butter: Unless specified, use unsalted butter wherever butter is called for.

Oiling and flouring pans: Use real butter when oiling and preparing a cake pan. Not only does the butter impart flavor, but it also makes a nice crust on the outside of the cake. Instead of using flour to flour your cake pans when baking chocolate cakes, use a couple tablespoons of the dry cake mix or cocoa powder. The finished cake won't have white streaks from the flour.

Testing cakes for doneness: Insert a toothpick into the center of the cake. If it comes out clean the cake is done. For thicker cake layers a bamboo skewer works well.

Cooling cakes: Let cakes cool out of the oven for at least 10 to 15 minutes in the cake pan on a rack. Then, when cakes have cooled somewhat, you should remove them to cooling racks until completely cool.

Note: Please read each and every chapter opener as there are numerous helpful hints, tips, and tricks to know for fast, fabulous results when making a delicious *Semi-Homemade*® dessert.

15

SHERRY TEA CAKES

Forget the crumpets—these lovely little tea cakes are the height of high style. Traditional yellow cupcakes, spiked with a subtle shot of cream sherry and frosted with delightfully drippy icing are effortless to make, yet so elegant to serve. Pair them with tall glasses of mint-sprigged iced tea in the summer and pretty china cups of hot tea in the winter. To create an instant tea party, script "tea" on each cake with blue decorator icing. For the holidays, try "noel" and "joy" in red and green; for a shower, try "baby" or "bride" and "groom" in pretty pastels. Stack the cakes on a tiered stand for a charming centerpiece, then match plates and table linens to the icing to pull it all together.

Makes 24 cupcakes

TEA CAKES:

1	box (18.25-ounce) yellow cake mix, *Duncan Hines Moist Deluxe®*
1	box (3.4-ounce) vanilla instant pudding and pie filling mix, *Jell-O®*
3/4	cup cream sherry, *Gallo®*
3/4	cup vegetable oil
4	eggs
3/4	teaspoon ground nutmeg, *McCormick®*

SHERRY GLAZE:

4	cups confectioners/powdered sugar
1/2	cup cream sherry, *Gallo®*
	Blue decorating gel (or other desired color)

Prep time:	12 minutes
Baking time:	18 minutes
Cooling time:	20 minutes
Frosting time:	15 minutes

Tea Cakes Preparation:

Preheat oven to 350 degrees.
Line 24 muffin cups with paper liners.
Combine cake mix, pudding mix, sherry, oil, eggs, and nutmeg in large bowl.
Beat for 2 minutes, or until well blended.
Spoon batter into prepared muffin cups, filling each 2/3 full.
Bake for 18 minutes, or until light golden-brown on top.
Cool cupcakes completely on cooling rack.

Sherry Glaze Preparation:

Place confectioners/powdered sugar in large bowl.
Gradually add sherry, stirring constantly until smooth.
Using small spatula or knife, frost each cupcake.
Once the sherry glaze is set, pipe decorating gel decoratively atop cupcakes.

PECAN CARAMEL CHEESECAKE

Pecan pie or cheesecake? Try a bite of both with this no-bake New York-style cheesecake smothered in caramelized pecans. The inspired combination of creamy cheesecake, gooey caramel, and crunchy pecans is a two-in-one treat, perfect for parties, special dinners or starting a new Thanksgiving tradition. Be generous with the caramel—and don't be afraid to let it drip down the sides. It just looks more homemade.

Serves 12 to 16

2	boxes (11.1 ounces each) real cheesecake dessert mix, *Jell-O No Bake®*
3/4	cup butter, melted
1/4	cup granulated sugar
2	tablespoons water
2 1/2	cups cold whole milk
1	cup butterscotch caramel sauce, *Mrs. Richardson's®*
1	cup pecans, toasted, chopped
1/2	cup golden brown sugar, packed

Prep time: 10 minutes
Chilling time: 5 hours

Preparation:

Line bottom of 9-inch-diameter springform pan with parchment or wax paper.
Mix 2 packages of crust, melted butter, sugar, and water in large bowl until well blended.
Reserve 1 cup of crumb mixture for topping.
Press remaining crumb mixture onto bottom of prepared pan (not up sides).
Combine 2 packages of cheesecake filling and cold milk in another large bowl.
Beat for 3 minutes, or until smooth and thick.
Fold 1/2 cup of caramel sauce into cheesecake mixture.
Pour mixture into crust-lined springform pan.
Mix reserved crumb mixture with 1/4 cup of caramel sauce, pecans, and brown sugar.
Sprinkle atop cheesecake.
Refrigerate cake at least 5 hours, or until set.
Run warm knife around pan sides to loosen cake; remove pan sides.
Transfer cake to serving platter and drizzle with remaining 1/4 cup of caramel sauce.
Serve cold.

from the package

WONTON NAPOLEONS

Serves 4

	Vegetable oil for frying
16	wonton wrappers (available in the refrigerated Asian foods section)
1 1/2	teaspoons ground cinnamon, *McCormick®*
2	cups frozen whipped topping, thawed, *Cool Whip®*
16	large strawberries, sliced
1	pint fresh raspberries
4	fresh mint sprigs (optional)

Prep time:	15 minutes
Assembly time:	10 minutes

Preparation:

Pour enough oil into small saucepan to come 1/4 inch up sides of pan.

Heat oil over medium-low heat.

Using tongs and working with 1 wonton at a time, submerge wontons into hot oil, frying until golden brown, about 15 seconds for first side and 10 seconds for second side.

Transfer fried wontons to paper towels to drain (wontons will continue to color slightly as they cool).

Sprinkle warm fried wontons with cinnamon.

Cool completely.

TO ASSEMBLE:

Place 4 fried wontons on work surface.

Spread 1 tablespoon of whipped topping over each.

Arrange 1 sliced strawberry and 2 to 3 raspberries over whipped topping on each wonton.

Spoon 1 tablespoon of whipped topping over berries on each wonton.

Top with another fried wonton.

Repeat layering 2 more times.

Spoon dollops of remaining whipped topping atop each cake stack.

Garnish napoleons with remaining strawberries and raspberries, and mint sprigs (optional).

Serve immediately.

TRIPLE LEMON POUND CAKE

Serves 8 to 10

CAKE:

1	box (18.25-ounce) lemon supreme cake mix, *Duncan Hines Moist Deluxe®*
1	box (3.9-ounce) lemon instant pudding and pie filling mix, *Jell-O®*
1	cup water
4	eggs
1/3	cup vegetable oil
	Zest of one lemon
6	tablespoons purchased lemon curd, stirred to loosen

LEMON GLAZE:

6	tablespoons purchased lemon curd, stirred to loosen
1/4	cup water
2	tablespoons fresh lemon juice
3	cups confectioners/powdered sugar

Prep time:	6 minutes
Baking time:	45 minutes
Cooling time:	30 minutes
Frosting time:	15 minutes

Preparation:

Preheat oven to 350 degrees.
Butter and flour 12-cup bundt pan or 13x9-inch metal baking pan.
Combine cake mix, pudding mix, water, eggs, oil, and lemon zest in large bowl.
Beat for 2 minutes, or until well blended.
Transfer batter to prepared pan.
Drizzle lemon curd atop batter, keeping curd away from sides of pan.
Bake for 45 minutes, or until toothpick inserted near center of cake comes out clean.
Cool cake in pan on cooling rack for 15 minutes.
Invert cake onto cooling rack. Place cooling rack atop cookie sheet.
Cool cake completely.

FOR THE LEMON GLAZE:

Beat curd, water, and lemon juice in large bowl until smooth.
Gradually add sugar, beating until mixture is smooth.
Drizzle glaze over cake.
Transfer cake to serving platter.

from the package

PHYLLO PIE BITES

Makes 12

8   plain phyllo pastry sheets (14x8-inch), thawed, *Athens®*
          Nonstick cooking spray, *PAM®*
3/4   cup cherry preserves, *Smucker's®*
2   tablespoons semi-sweet chocolate morsels, *Nestlé®*

Prep time: 20 minutes
Baking time: 20 minutes

Preparation:

Preheat oven to 375 degrees.
Line baking sheet with foil.
Place 1 phyllo sheet on work surface.
Spray phyllo sheet with cooking spray.
Top with second phyllo sheet and spray with cooking spray.
Repeat 2 more times, layering with 2 phyllo sheets and spraying each layer.
Cut stacked phyllo sheets into 6 even squares.
Spoon 1 scant tablespoon of cherry preserves into center of each square.
Sprinkle 1/2 teaspoon chocolate morsels over preserves.
Enclose filling by gathering phyllo and pinching tops tightly to form purses.
Transfer phyllo purses to prepared baking sheet.
Repeat with remaining 4 phyllo sheets, cooking spray, preserves, and chocolate morsels.
Bake for 20 minutes, or until phyllo is crisp and golden.
Cool pastries on cookie sheet.

CHOCOLATE POUND CAKE AND NEAPOLITAN BAKED ALASKA

My grandmother introduced me to Baked Alaska on an Alaskan cruise, and this delectable dessert has held a place in my heart ever since. A tongue-tingling mix of warm meringue and cold ice cream, it literally melts in your mouth. With a ready-made cake and ice cream, you can make this classic in just 15 minutes—then freeze it until it's ready to brown.

Serves 6 to 8

CAKE:

1	block carton (1/2 gallon) Neapolitan ice cream
4	1-inch-thick slices chocolate swirl pound cake, *Sara Lee®*

MERINGUE:

3	egg whites
1/2	teaspoon cream of tartar, *McCormick®*
1/3	cup granulated sugar

Prep time:	15 minutes
Freezing time:	4 hours

Preparation:

Line 8 1/2 x 4 1/2 x 2 1/2-inch metal loaf pan with 2 layers of plastic wrap, allowing 3 inches of plastic to hang over pan sides. Cut ice cream block crosswise in half, then lay ice cream halves cut side up in bottom of prepared pan, covering bottom of pan. Arrange cake slices atop ice cream, forming 1 even layer and covering ice cream completely. Fold plastic overhang atop cake to cover. Freeze for 4 hours, or until frozen solid. Wrap hot damp towels around pan sides to loosen cake and ice cream from pan. Fold back plastic from atop cake. Invert baking dish or large flame-proof plate atop cake. Holding baking dish and pan together, invert cake into dish. Remove pan; keep cake covered with plastic wrap. Freeze while preparing meringue.

TO SERVE:

Preheat oven to 450 degrees. Beat eggs whites in large clean bowl until frothy. Add cream of tartar to eggs and beat until soft peaks form. Gradually add sugar, beating until stiff peaks form. Remove plastic from cake. Spread meringue over cake, covering cake and ice cream completely and sealing meringue to dish. Bake until meringue is lightly brown and just set, about 3 minutes. Serve immediately.

SWEET SORBET SPRITZER

This colorful cocktail has all the shades of a Caribbean sunset…and the sultry indolence of a long summer night. A swirl of sweet mango, the festive fizz of ginger ale, and a splash of smooth sorbet combine in a kick-back cooler as light and refreshing as an island breeze. Grab a couple of goblets, throw off your shoes, and drink in the allure of the islands… wherever you happen to be. This drink is nirvana in a glass.

Serves 4

1	cup canned mango nectar, chilled, *Kern's®*
1	pint mango sorbet, *Häagen-Dazs®*
1	pint strawberry sorbet, *Dreyer's®* or *Edy's®*
2	cups ginger ale, chilled, *Canada Dry®*

Prep time: 5 minutes

Preparation:

Divide mango nectar among 4 chilled glasses. Scoop sorbets into glasses. Slowly pour ginger ale over sorbets. Drink immediately.

MANGO MARGARITAS

Serves 2

	Sugar
1/2	lime, cut into quarters
1/2	cup tequila
2/3	cup mango nectar, *Kern's®*
3	tablespoons bottled lime juice, *ReaLemon®*
1	cup medium ice cubes

Prep Time: 5 minutes

Preparation:

Spread thin layer of sugar on a saucer. Run 1 lime wedge around rim of each of 2 margarita or martini glasses. Press rims into sugar on saucer to created narrow sugared edge on each glass. In a cocktail shaker or small pitcher, combine tequila, mango nectar, lime juice, and ice cubes. Shake or stir vigorously for 30 seconds. Strain equal amounts into each glass. Squeeze juice from 1 lime piece into each drink and drop lime piece in. Serve immediately.

Note: For a nonalcoholic margarita, omit tequila, reduce ice cubes to 1/2 cup, place mango nectar, lime juice, and ice cubes in blender set on frappe and process until smooth.

HELPFUL HINTS, TIPS, AND TRICKS

Melting chocolate notes: Stir dark or milk chocolate as it melts to keep it smooth. If the cocoa butter crystals in the chocolate come in contact with any moisture during melting they may cause the chocolate to seize. For this reason, never cover chocolate when melting; moisture may get trapped inside the bowl or pot and drip back into the chocolate, causing it to seize. The same can happen if the chocolate is melted over rapidly simmering or boiling water, which causes steam. If the chocolate seizes, try stirring a teaspoon of oil for every 12 ounces of chocolate into it, but this trick may not work and the only remedy is to start over.

Melting chocolate in the microwave: For chocolate morsels, place morsels in a glass bowl and microwave on medium power at 30-second intervals, stirring between intervals. The chocolate is done when it looks shiny and stirs easily into a smooth pool.

Melting chocolate over a double boiler: You can use a conventional double boiler or a pot with a stainless steel bowl set on top. Fill bottom pot with a few inches of water and bring to a very gentle simmer. The water should not touch the bottom of the bowl or upper pot or the chocolate might scorch. Stir frequently until the chocolate melts completely and is very smooth.

Note: Please read each and every chapter opener as there are numerous helpful hints, tips, and tricks to know for fast, fabulous results when making a delicious *Semi-Homemade*® dessert.

from the chocolatier

CHOCOLATE THUMBPRINT COOKIES

Makes about 48 cookies

1	container (16-ounce) dark chocolate frosting, *Betty Crocker Rich & Creamy*®
1/2	stick butter, room temperature
2 1/2	cups graham cracker crumbs, *Nabisco Honey Maid*®
1/2	teaspoon pure almond extract, *McCormick*®
1	cup very finely ground almonds
48	(about) chocolate Kisses, unwrapped, *Hershey's*®

Prep time: 25 minutes
Chilling time: 30 minutes

Preparation:

Beat chocolate frosting and butter in large bowl until well blended.
Mix in graham cracker crumbs and almond extract.
Place almonds in pie pan or other shallow bowl.
Shape chocolate mixture into 1-inch balls.
Roll each ball in very finely ground almonds to coat.
Place balls on cookie sheet.
Using finger, make deep indentation in center of each ball.
Fill indentations with chocolate Kisses.
Refrigerate for 30 minutes, or until cold.

FROZEN ENGLISH TOFFEE CAKE

Serves 12 to 16

CAKE:

1	box (18.25-ounce) devil's food cake mix, *Duncan Hines Moist Deluxe*®
1 1/3	cups water
1/2	cup vegetable oil
3	eggs

ICE CREAM FILLING AND FROSTING:

1/2	gallon chocolate or vanilla ice cream, softened, *Dreyers*® or *Edy's*®
1	bag (10-ounce) English toffee bits, *SKOR*®
1	container (8-ounce) frozen whipped topping, thawed, *Cool Whip*®

Prep time:	15 minutes
Baking time:	30 minutes
Cooling time:	30 minutes
Freezing time:	3 hours

Cake Preparation:

Preheat oven to 350 degrees. Butter and flour two 8-inch-round cake pans. Combine cake mix, water, oil, and eggs in large bowl. Beat for 2 minutes, or until well blended. Pour batter into prepared pans. Bake for 30 minutes, or until toothpick inserted into center of cakes comes out clean. Cool cakes in pans on cooling rack for 15 minutes. Remove cakes from pans and cool cakes completely on cooling rack.

Ice Cream Filling Preparation:

Line three 8-inch-round cake pans with plastic wrap, allowing 3 inches of plastic to hang over sides. Divide ice cream equally among pans. Using rubber spatula, spread ice cream over bottoms of prepared pans, forming smooth, even layers. Sprinkle 1/4 cup of toffee bits over ice cream in each pan. Freeze for 3 hours, or until frozen solid.

TO ASSEMBLE AND FROST:

Cut each cake layer horizontally in half. Working quickly, remove ice cream from pans. Peel off plastic and place 1 ice cream circle on each of 3 cake layers. Stack cake and ice cream layers atop each other on serving platter. Top with remaining cake layer. Frost cake with whipped topping and sprinkle with remaining toffee bits. Freeze until ready to serve. Let ice cream cake stand at room temperature for 5 minutes before serving.

VIENNESE ICE CREAM CAKE

Serves 8 to 10

2	packages (5.5 ounces each; 20 sticks total) chocolate caramel cookie bars, *Twix®*
1	quart coffee ice cream, softened, *Häagen-Dazs®*
3/4	cup butterscotch caramel topping, *Mrs. Richardson's®*
3/4	cup chopped pecans, toasted
1	quart vanilla ice cream, softened, *Dreyer's®* or *Edy's®*
1	container (8-ounce) frozen whipped topping, thawed, *Cool Whip®*
1	(1.55-ounce) milk chocolate candy bar, shaved, *Hershey's®*

Special equipment:
Pastry bag (or resealable storage bag)
#6 star tip

Prep time:	40 minutes
Freezing time:	4 hours

Preparation:

Line 9 1/4 x 5 x 2 3/4-inch metal loaf pan with 2 layers of plastic wrap, allowing 3 inches of plastic to hang over pan sides. Stand cookies along sides of prepared pan, spacing evenly. Using rubber spatula, press 1/4 of coffee ice cream into pan. Drizzle 1 tablespoon of caramel topping over ice cream. Sprinkle 1 tablespoon of pecans over caramel. Spread 1/4 of vanilla ice cream over nuts. Drizzle 1 tablespoon of caramel topping over ice cream. Sprinkle 1 tablespoon of pecans over caramel. Freeze 20 minutes, or until firm. Repeat layering coffee ice cream, caramel, pecans and vanilla ice cream 3 more times, freezing for 20 minutes between each layering. Fold plastic overhang atop cake to cover. Freeze for 4 hours, or until frozen solid.

TO UNMOLD:

Wrap hot damp towels around pan to loosen ice cream cake from pan. Fold back plastic from atop ice cream cake. Invert large plate or serving platter atop ice cream cake. Holding plate and pan together, invert cake onto plate. Remove pan from cake; peel off plastic wrap. Spoon whipped topping into pastry bag fitted with star tip. Pipe stripes or fluted lines atop cake. Freeze 1 hour, or until whipped topping is frozen solid. Let cake stand at room temperature 10 minutes before serving. Sprinkle chocolate shavings over cake. Cut cake crosswise into slices; transfer cake slices to plates.

CRISPY ORANGE COCONUT BALLS

Crunchy milk chocolate with an undertone of orange and a coating of crisp coconut make these bite-size balls the dessert to serve when you're looking for something a bit different…and a bit more fun. Stack them in individual parfait glasses or in playful coconut-shell goblets to liven up your tablescape, or heap them in a serve-yourself basket for a buffet. To hand them out as party favors, slip a handful into a decorative bag or box, tie with a colorful ribbon and send your guests home with sweet memories of the evening.

Makes about 2 dozen

1	container (16-ounce) dark chocolate fudge or milk chocolate frosting, *Duncan Hines Creamy Homestyle®*
2 3/4	cups confectioners/powdered sugar, sifted
2	teaspoons pure orange extract, *McCormick®*
1 1/2	cups chocolatey sweetened rice cereal, *Kellogg's Cocoa Rice Crispies®*
2	cups sweetened flaked coconut, toasted, *Baker's®*

Prep time: 30 minutes

Preparation:

Line cookie sheet with wax paper.

Beat frosting and sifted confectioners/powdered sugar in large bowl until well blended.

Beat in orange extract. Stir in rice cereal.

Using tablespoon or 1-ounce cookie scoop, shape mixture into balls and place on cookie sheet.

Cover and refrigerate for 20 minutes, or until slightly firm.

Roll balls in coconut to coat.

Cover and refrigerate until ready to serve.

FROZEN COOKIE CAKE

Serves 12 to 16

CAKE:

1	box (18.25-ounce) devil's food cake mix, *Duncan Hines Moist Deluxe®*
1 1/2	cups water
1/2	cup vegetable oil
3	eggs

GANACHE AND FILLING:

1	cup heavy cream
1	bag (12-ounce) semi-sweet chocolate morsels, *Nestlé®*
1/2	gallon cookies 'n cream ice cream, softened, *Dreyers®* or *Edy's®*

Prep time: 10 minutes, baking time: 25 minutes, cooling time: 30 minutes
Chilling time: 1 hour, freezing time: 3 hours

Cake Preparation:

Preheat oven to 350 degrees. Butter and flour two 10-inch-round cake pans. Combine cake mix, water, oil, and eggs in large bowl. Beat for 2 minutes, or until well blended. Divide batter between prepared pans. Bake for 25 minutes, or until toothpick inserted into center of cakes comes out clean. Cool cakes in pans on cooling rack for 15 minutes. Remove cakes from pans and cool cakes completely on cooling rack.

Ganache Preparation:

Heat cream in small saucepan until small bubbles appear around edge. Remove pan from heat. Add chocolate morsels and stir until ganache mixture is smooth. Refrigerate ganache until cool and slightly thickened, stirring occasionally, about 30 minutes. Spread ganache over top and sides of cakes. Refrigerate cakes for 1 hour, or until ganache is set.

Filling Preparation:

Line one 9-inch-round cake pan with plastic wrap, allowing 3 inches of plastic to hang over pan sides. Using rubber spatula, spread ice cream over prepared pan, forming smooth, even layer. Freeze for 3 hours, or until frozen solid.

To Assemble:

Place 1 cake layer, ganache side up, on serving platter. Remove ice cream circle from pan, peel off plastic. Place ice cream circle atop cake. Top with second cake layer, ganache side up. Freeze until ready to serve. Let finished cake stand at room temperature for 5 minutes before serving.

Variation: Use a wooden skewer to write and decorate ganache atop cake to make this cake look even more like an cookie.

CHOCOLATE BUNDT CAKE
WITH CHOCOLATE GANACHE FROSTING

Ganache is a smooth mixture of melted chocolate and cream that hardens to a glossy glaze. Drizzle it over a moist, spongy bundt cake for a dressy dessert that pairs perfectly with coffee. It's a gorgeous treat for company or an ideal indulgence any time of day—breakfast, brunch, or dinner.

Serves 8 to 10

CAKE:

1	box (18.25-ounce) Swiss chocolate cake mix, *Duncan Hines Moist Deluxe®*
1	box (3.9-ounce) chocolate instant pudding and pie filling mix, *Jell-O®*
1	cup water
4	eggs
1/3	cup vegetable oil
1/2	cup (4 ounces) semi-sweet chocolate morsels, *Nestlé®*

GANACHE:

1	cup heavy cream
1	package (12-ounce) semi-sweet chocolate morsels, *Nestlé®*
	Additional semi-sweet chocolate morsels, *Nestlé®* (optional)

Prep time:	8 minutes
Baking time:	45 minutes
Cooling time:	40 minutes
Frosting time:	15 minutes

Cake Preparation:

Preheat oven to 350 degrees. Butter and flour 12-cup bundt pan. Combine cake mix, pudding mix, water, eggs, and oil in large bowl. Beat for 2 minutes, or until well blended. Stir in 1/2 cup of chocolate morsels. Transfer batter to prepared bundt pan. Bake for 45 minutes, or until toothpick inserted near center of cake comes out clean. Cool cake in pan on cooling rack for 15 minutes. Invert cake onto cooling rack. Place cooling rack atop cookie sheet. Cool cake completely.

Ganache Preparation:

Heat cream in small saucepan over low heat until small bubbles appear. Remove from heat. Add chocolate morsels to cream and stir until smooth. Cool ganache just until it is slightly warm. Pour ganache over cooled cake, coating cake completely. Transfer cake to serving platter. Garnish with additional semi-sweet chocolate morsels (optional).

from the chocolatier

PEANUT BUTTER MINI MUD PIES

Makes 6

6   tablespoons creamy peanut butter, *Jif®*
6   mini graham cracker crusts, *Keebler Ready Crust®*
3 1/2 cups (from 1 quart) coffee ice cream, *Häagen-Dazs®*
1   bottle (7-ounce) milk chocolate shell topping, *Hershey's®*
1   tablespoon graham cracker crumbs, *Nabisco Honey Maid®*

Prep time: 10 minutes
Freezing time: 1 hour

Preparation:

Spread 1 tablespoon of peanut butter into bottom of each crust.
Using 1/2-cup or 4-ounce ice cream scoop, place ball of ice cream into each crust.
Freeze for at least 1 hour, or until ice cream and crusts are frozen solid.
Remove pies from foil pie tins; place pies on plates.
Drizzle milk chocolate shell topping over ice cream in crusts.
Immediately sprinkle 1/2 teaspoon of crumbs over each pie and serve.

*Variation: To make mini chocolate pie crusts (as shown in the photo), scrape the filling from Oreo®
cookies, then finely grind the cookies in a food processor. Mix the crumbs with just enough melted
butter to moisten lightly. Press the crumb mixture over the sides and bottom of mini pie pans.*

from the chocolatier

WHITE CHOCOLATE MACADAMIA NUT BARK

Makes 1 1/2 pounds

CANDY:

2	cups semi-sweet chocolate morsels, *Nestlé®*
2	cups vanilla milk white chips, *Guittard Choc-Au-Lait®*
2/3	cup toasted macadamia nuts or toasted almonds, coarsely chopped

Prep time:	10 minutes
Chilling time:	30 minutes

Preparation:

Line 13x9-inch cookie sheet with wax paper, allowing 2 inches of paper to hang over sides. Melt all but 1/4 cup of semi-sweet chocolate morsels in microwave on medium power for 2 minutes, stirring every 30 seconds, or until smooth. Pour chocolate onto prepared sheet and spread to cover entire surface and form 1 even layer. Melt all but 1/4 cup of white chips in microwave on medium power for 2 minutes, stirring every 30 seconds, or until smooth. Drizzle melted white chips over semi-sweet chocolate layer. Using toothpick or skewer, swirl melted chocolates together, creating marbled effect. Sprinkle with nuts and remaining chocolate morsels and white chips. Gently press toppings into melted chocolates. Refrigerate for 30 minutes, or until chocolate is firm. Remove wax paper from chocolate. Cut or break chocolate into bite-size pieces.

ALMOND HAYSTACKS

Makes 12 pieces

1	bag (12-ounce) semi-sweet chocolate morsels, *Nestlé®*
2	cups slivered almonds, toasted

Prep time:	10 minutes
Chilling time:	20 minutes

Preparation:

Line cookie sheet with parchment paper or wax paper. Melt chocolate in microwave on medium power for 2 minutes, stirring every 30 seconds, or until smooth. Using 1 tablespoon of chocolate for each, spoon 12 chocolate circles onto prepared sheet, spacing evenly. Sprinkle each with 1 tablespoon of almonds. Refrigerate for 10 minutes, or until chocolate is firm. Rewarm chocolate and drizzle 1 teaspoon into center of each chocolate-nut circle. Top each with 1 teaspoon of almonds. Refrigerate for 10 minutes, or until chocolate is firm. Repeat layering 1 more time, adding as much height to stacks as possible.

From the American Classics

HELPFUL HINTS, TIPS, AND TRICKS

Frosting cakes: Frosting can become difficult to handle if it becomes too warm. If this happens, place the cake and frosting in the refrigerator for 10 minutes to chill.

When freezing cakes: After cakes have cooled completely, wrap tightly in plastic, then in aluminum foil. Cakes can be kept frozen for up to three months.

When freezing frosted cakes: If cakes are frosted, place them in the freezer until frosting is firm, then wrap them the same way as unfrosted cakes.

When thawing frozen cakes: Remove wrapping, then place cake in an airtight container. Allow cake to defrost in the refrigerator overnight, then bring it up to room temperature before serving.

Note: Please read each and every chapter opener as there are numerous helpful hints, tips, and tricks to know for fast, fabulous results when making a delicious *Semi-Homemade*® dessert.

PORT OF SAN FRANCISCO SUNDAE

This vintage childhood favorite looks like it's right out of *Willy Wonka and the Chocolate Factory* but with a grown-up twist—a brown sugar Port sauce and elegant white chocolate. Every bite brings a burst of flavors and textures—chunky chocolate, velvety hot fudge, sugary Port, and fluffy froths of whipped cream. I serve it in a clear goblet, so you can see how wonderfully the colors blend together. The recipe makes one cup of sauce—enough for four sundaes. If you really want to do it up, slip a chocolate-covered cherry on top (recipe on page 111).

Serves 4

PORT SAUCE:

2	cups ruby Port, *Christian Brothers®*
1 1/2	cups (packed) golden brown sugar

SUNDAE:

1	quart vanilla or chocolate chip ice cream, *Häagen-Dazs®*
1/2	cup chocolate hot fudge topping, warm, *Hershey's®*
1/4	cup premier white morsels, *Nestlé®*

Prep time:	10 minutes
Cooking time:	10 minutes

Port Sauce Preparation:

Bring Port and sugar to boil in heavy small saucepan over high heat.
Reduce heat and simmer for 10 minutes, or until mixture is syrupy.
Cool sauce slightly.

Sundae Preparation:

Scoop ice cream into 4 wineglasses or sundae dishes.
Spoon hot fudge sauce over ice cream, then spoon 1/4 cup of warm Port sauce over each sundae.
Sprinkle with white morsels.
Serve immediately.

Tip: Port Sauce can be made 1 day ahead. Cover and refrigerate. Rewarm in microwave.

SOUR CREAM PHILADELPHIA CHEESECAKE WITH CHERRIES

Serves 8

1	box (11.2-ounce) homestyle cheesecake dessert mix, *Jell-O No Bake®*
3/4	stick butter, melted
2	tablespoons granulated sugar
1 1/3	cups cold whole milk
1/3	cup sour cream
1	container (21-ounce) cherry pie filling or topping, *Comstock More Fruit®*

Prep time: 10 minutes, baking time: 10 minutes, chilling time: 30 minutes

Preparation:

Preheat oven to 350 degrees. Stir crumbs from cheesecake mix, melted butter, and sugar in large bowl until crumbs are moistened. Press crumb mixture over bottom of 9-inch-diameter spring-form pan. Bake until crust is set and golden brown around edges, about 10 minutes. Pat down crust. Refrigerate crust for 15 minutes, or until cooled completely. Combine cheesecake filling mix, milk, and sour cream in another large bowl. Beat for 2 minutes, or until smooth. Pour filling over crust. Refrigerate for 30 minutes, or until filling is set.

TO UNMOLD: Carefully remove sides from pan and place cheesecake on serving platter. Using sharp knife, cut cake into wedges; transfer to plates. Spoon cherry pie filling over and serve.

AWARD-WINNING NEW YORK BLINTZES

Serves 6

1	cup sour cream
2 1/2	tablespoons granulated sugar
1/2	cup cream cheese, room temperature, *Philadelphia®*
1 1/2	cups cherry pie filling or topping, *Comstock More Fruit®*
1/4	cup semi-sweet chocolate mini morsels, *Nestlé®*
1	teaspoon lemon zest
6	purchased 7-inch-square crêpes, *Frieda's®*, or 6 purchased 9-inch-diameter crêpes, *Melissa's®*
3	tablespoons butter

Prep time: 20 minutes

Preparation:

Mix sour cream and sugar in small bowl to blend. Beat cream cheese in large bowl until light and fluffy. Stir 1 cup cherry pie filling, chocolate morsels, and lemon zest into cream cheese. Place 1 crêpe on work surface, spoon 3 tablespoons of cream cheese mixture into center of crêpe. Fold bottom of crêpe over filling, and then fold opposite side of crêpe over. Repeat with remaining crêpes and cream cheese mixture. Melt 1 tablespoon of butter on large nonstick griddle over medium-low heat. Place 2 blintzes seam side down in hot butter. Fry for 2 minutes on each side, or until crêpes are golden and filling is heated through. Transfer blintzes to serving plates. Repeat with remaining blintzes, adding more butter to griddle as needed. Top with sweetened sour cream and remaining cherry pie filling, and serve.

Variations: Fold bottom of crêpe over filling. Fold in sides and roll up.

CHICAGO BREAD PUDDING
WITH CARAMEL RUM SAUCE

Chicago's humble bread pudding gets a tony twist when made with buttery brioche and a drizzle of caramel rum sauce. If you don't want to use rum, use rum or almond extract. To warm up a chilly midwestern winter evening, serve pudding in a brandy snifter with heated caramel sauce dripping down the sides. In the sultry summer, serve it chilled in a sundae dish. If you're short on time, the pudding can be made a day in advance.

Serves 8 to 10

BREAD PUDDING:

1	pound purchased brioche bread
5	cups cold whole milk
2	boxes (4.4 ounces each) Americana custard dessert mix, *Jell-O®*
1/3	cup dark rum, *Myers's®*
2	egg yolks, beaten to blend
1/4	teaspoon grated nutmeg, *McCormick®*
1/4	cup walnut pieces, lightly toasted
1/4	cup pecan pieces, lightly toasted
1/2	cup golden raisins, *Sun-Maid®* (optional)

CARAMEL RUM SAUCE:

3/4	cup butterscotch caramel sauce, *Mrs. Richardson's®*
3	tablespoons heavy cream
3	tablespoons dark rum, *Myers's®*

Prep time: 15 minutes
Baking time: 50 minutes

Bread Pudding Preparation:

Preheat oven to 350 degrees.
Butter 13x9-inch baking dish.
Tear brioche into 1-inch pieces and place in prepared dish.
Combine milk, custard dessert mix, rum, eggs, and nutmeg in large bowl.
Whisk until well blended. Stir in nuts and raisins (optional).
Pour over brioche; press brioche to submerge into custard.
Let set for 10 minutes, or until brioche absorbs custard slightly.
Bake for 50 minutes, or until top is golden brown and bread pudding puffs.
Serve warm with Caramel Rum Sauce.

Caramel Rum Sauce Preparation:

Combine caramel sauce, cream, and rum in medium glass bowl.
Heat in microwave for 45 seconds. Whisk to blend.

Note: Sauce can also be served cold. Cover and refrigerate sauce until cold.

BOSTON CREAM PIE

Serves 8

CAKE AND FILLING:
I 1/4   cups cold whole milk
I   box (3.4-ounce) vanilla instant pudding and pie filling mix, *Jell-O®*
I   tablespoon pure vanilla extract, *McCormick®*
I   box (16-ounce) pound cake, *Entenmann's®*

GLAZE:
1/2   cup chocolate hot fudge topping, *Hershey's®*
1/4   cup confectioners/powdered sugar, sifted

Prep time: 25 minutes
Chilling time: I hour

Preparation:

Combine milk, instant pudding mix, and vanilla in large bowl.
Beat for 2 minutes, or until pudding thickens.
Refrigerate for 15 minutes.
Line 2-quart loaf pan with 2 layers of plastic wrap, allowing 2 inches of plastic to hang over sides.
Cut pound cake horizontally to make 3 equal layers.
Place I cake layer in bottom of prepared pan.
Spread half of pudding evenly over cake.
Top with second cake layer; spread with remaining pudding.
Top with third cake layer.
Fold plastic overhang atop cake to cover.
Refrigerate cake for I hour before serving.

FOR THE GLAZE:
Stir chocolate fudge sauce and confectioners/powdered sugar in medium bowl until smooth.
Fold back plastic from atop cake.
Using plastic as aid, lift cake from pan; remove plastic.
Cut cake crosswise into slices.
Transfer cake slices to plates.
Spoon glaze over cake and serve.

TEXAS CINNAMON PECAN STRUDEL

Makes 10 to 12 slices

1	package (18-ounce) frozen unbaked cinnamon rolls, thawed, *Rich's®*
3	tablespoons honey, *Sue Bee®*
1/2	cup chopped pecans
1/2	cup chopped walnuts
	Additional honey, *Sue Bee®*
1	teaspoon ground cinnamon, *McCormick®*

Prep time:	10 minutes
Baking time:	20 minutes

Preparation:

Preheat oven to 375 degrees.

Line cookie sheet with parchment paper.

Gather cinnamon rolls into one ball.

Knead dough in bowl until smooth.

Roll out dough on lightly floured work surface to 12x7-inch rectangle.

Brush dough with 3 tablespoons honey.

Sprinkle dough with pecans and walnuts.

Gently press nuts into dough.

Roll up dough as for jelly roll.

Place dough seamside down on prepared cookie sheet.

Bake for 20 minutes, or until golden brown.

Cut strudel crosswise into diagonal slices.

Drizzle with additional honey and sprinkle with cinnamon.

Serve warm.

COLORADO CHOCOLATE PEAKS

Makes 20

CAKE:

1 1/3	cups water
2	tablespoons instant coffee crystals, *Maxwell House®*
1	box (18.3-ounce) chocolate fudge cake mix, *Betty Crocker SuperMoist®*
1/3	cup vegetable oil
3	eggs
20	soft caramel candies, unwrapped, *Brach's Milk Maid®*

FROSTING:

1	container (16-ounce) chocolate frosting, *Betty Crocker Rich & Creamy®*
1	jar (7-ounce) marshmallow creme, refrigerated, *Kraft Jet-Puffed®*
1/4	cup unsweetened cocoa powder, *Hershey's®*
1/4	cup sweetened flaked coconut, toasted, *Baker's®*

Prep time: 30 minutes, baking time: 12 minutes, cooling time: 15 minutes

Preparation:
Preheat oven to 350 degrees. Butter and flour two 6-cup cupcake pans. Stir 1 1/3 cups water and coffee crystals in large bowl until crystals dissolve. Let cool. Add cake mix, oil, and eggs to coffee in large bowl. Beat 2 minutes, or until well blended. Fill each muffin cup halfway with batter. Place 1 caramel in center of each. Pour remaining batter over caramels. Bake for 12 minutes, or until cakes have puffed up. Cool cupcakes in pans on racks for 15 minutes. Carefully remove cupcakes from pans. FOR THE FROSTING: Cut off tops of cupcakes; reserve tops. Frost cupcake bottoms with chocolate frosting. Spoon 1 tablespoon of chilled marshmallow creme atop each frosted bottom. Replace cake tops on cake bottoms. Dust with cocoa powder, sprinkle with coconut, and serve.

SEATTLE MORNING COFFEE CAKE

Makes 12 to 16 slices

7	sweet dinner rolls, *King's Hawaiian®*
1	box (1-pound, 14-ounce) cinnamon swirl coffee cake mix, *Pillsbury®*
3/4	cup water
1/4	cup vegetable oil
3	eggs
1	cup whole milk
1	tablespoon granulated sugar

Prep time: 10 minutes, baking time: 45 minutes, cooling time: 25 minutes

Preparation:
Preheat oven to 350 degrees. Butter and flour 10-cup bundt pan. Slice 1 inch off tops of rolls. Tear tops into 1-inch pieces; set aside. Place bottoms of rolls cutside up in prepared pan. Combine coffee cake batter mix, water, oil, and 2 eggs in large bowl. Beat until well blended. Pour half of batter over rolls. Sprinkle with contents of cinnamon swirl packet. Pour remaining batter over rolls. Whisk remaining 1 egg, milk, and sugar in another bowl to blend. Add reserved roll tops to milk mixture; set aside until milk mixture is absorbed. Pour bread mixture over cake batter in pan. Using skewer or wooden chopstick, swirl batters together. Bake for 45 minutes, or until toothpick inserted near center of cake comes out clean. Cool cake in pan on cooling rack for 25 minutes. Invert cake onto cooling rack; remove pan. Place cake right side up on platter and serve warm. For a cute presentation, serve slices in coffee mugs.

From the Stars

MAKING A DIFFERENCE

While creating this chapter, I was amazed to learn that these talented personalities seen on TV, stage, and the "Big Screen" have lives surprisingly similar to yours and mine. They're busy working people with families that depend on them, responsibilities that consume them, and convictions that drive them. They cook and clean, decorate their homes, go to work, and entertain friends. They're simply everyday people with high-profile jobs; thoughtful and caring, they lend their time and support to causes that help their communities and those less fortunate. They, like us, know that one person can make a difference and how much bigger that difference will be if we all chip in.

These two worthy organizations make a difference every day:

• Founded in 1989, Project Angel Food prepares and delivers more than 1,000 free meals daily to men, women, and children disabled by HIV/AIDS and other terminal illnesses, such as diabetes, cancer, and Parkinson's. In Project Angel Food's kitchen, you can find Eric McCormack cooking, Queen Latifah directing, Anthony Edwards serving, and Kristin Davis acting as sous chef. To lend your own helping hands, please visit PAF's website at www.angelfood.org or call 1-800-59-ANGEL.

• In 2000, the National Colorectal Cancer Research Alliance (NCCRA) was co-founded by Katie Couric, Lilly Tartikoff, and the Entertainment Industry Foundation (EIF) to raise awareness and research dollars in the fight against colon cancer. Katie lost her husband Jay Monahan to the disease in 1998 when he was 42 years old. The NCCRA supports cutting-edge research conducted by leading scientists that has already produced significant advances. For more information, visit the NCCRA or EIF Web sites at www.nccra.org or www.eifoundation.org or call 1-800-872-3000.

"When you learn…teach. When you get…give."

—From Oprah Winfrey's acceptance speech, 2002 Emmy Awards

KATIE COURIC'S EARLY MORNING RASPBERRY CRESCENT RING

Serves 12

CRESCENT RING:

2	containers (8 ounces each) refrigerated crescent roll dough, *Pillsbury*®
1	container (7-ounce) pure almond paste, *Odense*®
1/4	cup seedless red raspberry jam or cherry jam

GLAZE:

1	cup confectioners/powdered sugar
1 1/2	tablespoons water
1/4	teaspoon pure almond extract, *McCormick*®
	Sugar-dipped cherries and small pears (optional)

Prep time:	20 minutes
Baking time:	25 minutes
Cooling time:	10 minutes

Preparation:

Preheat oven to 375 degrees. Line heavy large baking sheet with parchment paper. Unroll crescent dough; separate along dough perforations into 16 triangles. Overlap 8 dough triangles on prepared baking sheet, positioning longest points in center and forming 10-inch-diameter dough disc. Press edges of triangles together to seal. Using rolling pin, roll out almond paste between 2 sheets of waxed paper into 9-inch-diameter disc. Remove plastic wrap and place almond paste disc atop dough disc. Spread jam over almond paste. Using remaining 8 dough triangles, arrange second 10-inch-diameter dough disc atop jam. Pinch edges of dough discs to seal. Tuck edges under. Bake for 25 minutes, or until golden brown. Remove from oven and cool for 10 minutes.

FOR THE GLAZE:

Stir confectioners/powdered sugar, water, and almond extract in medium bowl until smooth. Drizzle half of glaze over warm crescent. Let glaze set for 10 minutes. Drizzle remaining glaze over.

Note: Decorate with sugar-dipped cherries and small pears (optional).

PHOTO: MATT BARON/BEIMAGES

The day starts early for Katie Couric. By the time most of us roll out of bed, Katie's already been on the job for hours—and will be there for many more. Two young children and long workdays mean every minute counts in Katie's hectic household. Fortunately, this easy-bake breakfast ring will get anyone's morning off to a fruitful start. The shortcut is refrigerated crescent dough, filled with raspberry jam, and drizzled with an elegant almond glaze. Perfect for today—or any day.

ERIC McCORMACK'S AMAZING CHOCOLATE ALMOND BISCOTTI

Makes about 28 biscotti

1	box (18.25-ounce) dark chocolate fudge or devil's food cake mix, *Duncan Hines Moist Deluxe®*
1	cup all purpose flour
1	stick butter, melted
2	eggs
2	teaspoons pure almond extract, *McCormick®*
3/4	cup whole almonds

Prep time:	10 minutes
Baking time:	1 hour 30 minutes
Cooling time:	1 hour

Preparation:

Preheat oven to 350 degrees. Line 2 heavy large baking sheets with parchment paper. Combine cake mix, flour, melted butter, eggs, and almond extract in large bowl. Beat for 2 minutes, or until dough forms. Knead almonds into dough. Scrape dough onto 1 prepared baking sheet and form dough into 13-inch-long log that is 3 inches wide. Bake for 35 minutes, or until toothpick inserted into center of biscotti comes out clean. Cool for 35 minutes. Using serrated knife, cut log crosswise into 1/2-inch-thick slices. Carefully transfer half of biscotti to second prepared baking sheet. Arrange biscotti cut side down on baking sheets. Bake for 15 minutes. Reduce heat to 200 degrees. Bake for 40 minutes, or until biscotti are dry. Cool completely (biscotti will harden as they cool).

Variation: Melt dark or white chocolate, then dip bottoms of biscotti into chocolate to coat. Transfer biscotti to wax paper; set aside until chocolate becomes firm.

NBC PHOTO: CHRIS HASTON

Eric McCormack loves food. After all, the Will & Grace star lured his wife into marriage with his "Love Salad" recipe—just think what he can do with biscotti! The irresistible pairing of deep, dark chocolate and smoky almond is sure to steal hearts, and it's amazingly easy to make—a must when you have a new baby and a hit TV show requiring long days on the set. Who knows? This stylish snack might make a guest appearance in Will Truman's kitchen.

Join Emmy winner Eric for a night of laughs—and possibly dessert—on NBC's Will & Grace.

ANJELICA HUSTON'S HAVING-IT-ALL CARAMEL SHORTBREAD

Makes 16 pieces

1	box (5.3-ounce) pure butter shortbread triangles, *Walkers®*
20	soft caramel candies, unwrapped, *Brach's Milk Maid®*
1	tablespoon whole milk
1/2	cup chopped walnuts, toasted
1	cup semi-sweet chocolate morsels, *Nestlé®*

Prep time: 15 minutes

PHOTO: PLATON

Anjelica Huston wears many hats—actor, director, and producer—so it comes as no surprise that she's been known to don a chef's hat as well. From cooking one-pot meals like soup for her husband, sculptor Robert Graham, to indulging them both with grab-and-go treats, Anjelica knows that the secret to having it all is to keep it simple, especially in the kitchen. These quick cookies are a multitasker's delight—as tasty with coffee for breakfast as they are for a mid-day—or midnight—snack.

Check out Anjelica's Academy Award®-winning performance in Prizzi's Honor *or her wickedly funny turn in* The Addams Family.

Preparation:

Line cookie sheet with parchment paper. Place triangles on cookie sheet, spacing evenly apart. Combine caramels and milk in small microwavable bowl. Melt in microwave on medium power for 1 1/2 minutes, stirring every 30 seconds, or until smooth. Drizzle melted caramel over shortbread. Cool caramel slightly, then sprinkle with walnuts. Gently press walnuts into caramel. Melt chocolate morsels in microwave on medium power for 2 1/2 minutes, stirring every 30 seconds, or until melted and smooth. Dip shortbread into melted chocolate, covering half of each shortbread. Set shortbread aside on prepared cookie sheet until chocolate is firm. Store in airtight container at room temperature.

Variation: Substitute the semi-sweet chocolate morsels with premier white morsels. Dip half of the shortbread cookies in melted white morsels for two varieties.

QUEEN LATIFAH'S SILKY SMOOTH APRICOT MINI CAKES

Makes 36 bite-size cakes

36	dried apricots, *Sunsweet®*
4	ounces cream cheese, room temperature, *Philadelphia®*
3	tablespoons confectioners/powdered sugar
1/2	cup finely chopped walnuts, toasted
1	box (18.25-ounce) classic yellow cake mix, *Duncan Hines Moist Deluxe®*
1 1/3	cups water
1/3	cup vegetable oil
3	eggs
2	teaspoons pure almond extract, *McCormick®*
	Additional confectioners/powdered sugar (optional)

Special equipment:
Pastry bag and three 12-cup mini-cupcake pans

Prep time:	20 minutes
Baking time:	15 minutes
Cooling time:	15 minutes

Preparation:

Preheat oven to 350 degrees. Butter and flour mini-cupcake pans. Using kitchen shears or small sharp knife, cut 1/4-inch piece off 1 end of each apricot. Insert handle of wooden spoon into slit of each apricot to form pocket; set aside. Beat cream cheese in large bowl until light and fluffy. Beat in 3 tablespoons confectioners/powdered sugar. Mix in walnuts. Spoon cream cheese mixture into pastry bag without metal tip. Pipe cream cheese mixture into pockets of prepared apricots. Place 1 filled apricot into each cup of prepared mini-cupcake pans. Combine cake mix, water, oil, eggs, and almond extract in large bowl. Beat for 2 minutes, or until well blended. Spoon 1 tablespoon of batter over each apricot in pans. Bake for 15 minutes, or until lightly golden. Cool cakes completely in pans on cooling racks. Arrange cakes apricot side up on serving platter. Dust with additional confectioners/powdered sugar (optional).

Queen Latifah is a sweet surprise. In the film Chicago, *her silky smooth voice is an unexpected treat, as is her commitment to mentoring young girls. Even her name is a revelation—Latifah means delicate and sensitive in Arabic. These charming little cakes are another delicious discovery, with a delicacy and sweet surprise all their own. The apricot is baked on the bottom—just flip them over to reveal a delightful fruit center. They're soft, sweet, and soothing, just like our Queen L.*

See Grammy® winner Queen Latifah in the film Bringing Down the House *(she executive-produced it, too) or catch her Academy Award®-nominated performance in* Chicago.

NATHAN LANE'S FABULOUS FRIED ICE CREAM

Serves 4

1	quart vanilla ice cream, *Häagen-Dazs*®
5	cups honey crunch corn flakes, *Kellogg's*®
2	teaspoons ground cinnamon, *McCormick*®
2	eggs
	Canola oil for frying
4	tablespoons honey, *Sue Bee*®
1/2	cup frozen whipped topping, thawed, *Cool Whip*® (optional)

Prep time:	15 minutes
Freezing time:	3 hours
Cooking time:	4 minutes

Preparation:

Scoop 8 balls of ice cream and place 1/2 inch apart on cake pan(s). Freeze for 3 hours, or until ice cream is frozen solid. Combine corn flakes and cinnamon in large resealable plastic bag; seal bag. Using rolling pin, crush corn flakes into crumbs. Transfer crumb mixture to large bowl. Removing 1 ice cream ball at a time from freezer, roll ice cream balls in crumb mixture, pressing crumbs onto ice cream to coat completely. Freeze ice cream balls until frozen solid. Beat eggs in medium bowl to blend. Working with 1 ice cream ball at a time, dip balls into egg, turning to coat, then roll balls in crumb mixture, pressing crumb mixture to coat ice cream balls again. Return ice cream balls to freezer until ready to fry.

TO FRY ICE CREAM:

Add enough oil to large deep saucepan to come halfway up sides of pan. Heat oil over medium-high heat to about 300 degrees. Using fryer basket or slotted spoon, add 2 ice cream balls to hot oil. Fry for 1 minute, or just until coating is crisp. Using slotted spoon, remove ice cream balls from oil and place on paper towel to drain excess oil. Transfer ice cream balls to dessert dish or cup. Drizzle with 1 tablespoon of honey and dollop with whipped topping (optional). Serve immediately. Repeat frying with remaining ice cream balls.

PHOTO: TIMOTHY WHITE

Flamboyant funnyman Nathan Lane has mastered stage, screen, and television. What's next? The kitchen! "The Man Who Came to Dinner" has a soft spot for dessert, especially ice cream fried to a delectable crunch. This sumptuous scene stealer is a fiesta of flavors—warm and crispy on the outside, cool and creamy on the inside. Serve it in a tall, cool parfait glass for a south-of-the-border treat just north of nirvana.

If you missed Nathan's Tony Award®-winning performance in The Producers, *you can rent his classic comic turns in* The Birdcage *and* Mouse Hunt.

SHARON STONE'S SEXY SWEET CHOCOLATE LAYER CAKE

Serves 12 to 14

1   box (18.25-ounce) Swiss chocolate cake mix, *Duncan Hines Moist Deluxe®*
2 1/2 cups water
1   cup vegetable oil
6   eggs
1   box (18.25-ounce) classic white cake mix, *Duncan Hines Moist Deluxe®*
1   container (16-ounce) rich and creamy dark chocolate frosting, *Betty Crocker Rich & Creamy®*
2   containers (12 ounces each) fluffy white frosting, *Betty Crocker Whipped®*

OPTIONAL CHOCOLATE CURLS:
1 bar (8-ounce) white chocolate, *Lindt®*

Prep time: 10 minutes, baking time: 30 minutes,
Cooling time: 30 minutes, frosting time: 25 minutes

Preparation:

Preheat oven to 350 degrees. Butter and flour four 8-inch-round cake pans. Combine chocolate cake mix, 1 1/4 cups water, 1/2 cup oil, and 3 eggs in large bowl. Beat for 2 minutes, or until well blended. Divide batter between 2 prepared cake pans. Combine white cake mix, remaining 1 1/4 cups water, 1/2 cup oil, and 3 eggs in another large bowl. Beat for 2 minutes, or until well blended. Divide batter between remaining 2 prepared cake pans. Bake for 30 minutes, or until toothpick inserted into center of cakes comes out clean. Cool cakes in pans on cooling rack for 15 minutes. Invert cakes onto cooling rack. Cool cakes completely. Using sharp or serrated knife, cut each cake horizontally in half, forming 8 layers total. Place 1 white cake layer cut side down on platter; spread 1/4 cup of dark chocolate frosting over top of cake. Place 1 chocolate cake layer cut side up atop first cake layer; spread 1/4 cup of white frosting over top of chocolate cake layer. Repeat layering and frosting until all layers are used. Frost entire cake with remaining white frosting. Refrigerate cake until ready to serve.

TO MAKE OPTIONAL CHOCOLATE CURLS:
Chocolate bars must be at room temperature. Using vegetable peeler, scrape 1 long side of chocolate bars, forming curls. Decorate top of cake with chocolate curls.

Style, grace, glamour—Sharon Stone has them all. The toast of Tinseltown, ever elegant Sharon, a devoted new mom, has shifted her priorities to focus on the sweeter side of life—life with young son Roan. For a dessert that sizzles with style, Sharon chooses this luxuriously luscious layer cake. It's the stuff of fantasy—layer upon layer of sweetly sensual chocolate and white cake, stacked with stripes of fluffy frosting in between and crowned with curls of rich white chocolate. It's a divine diva of a dessert—a dream to make...and serve.

See Sharon sizzle in her Oscar®-nominated role in Casino *and her romantic romp in* The Muse. *You can also see Sharon's layered performance in* Cold Creek Manor.

JAMIE LEE CURTIS' QUICK-BAKE BUTTERSCOTCH FUDGE

Makes 16 large or 32 small bars

1	box (18.25-ounce) devil's food cake mix, *Duncan Hines Moist Deluxe®*
1	cup extra crunchy peanut butter, *Jif®*
1/4	cup water
2	eggs
1	cup semi-sweet chocolate morsels, *Nestlé®*
1/2	cup chocolatey sweetened rice cereal, *Kellogg's Cocoa Rice Krispies®*
1	cup butterscotch morsels, *Nestlé®*

Prep time:	10 minutes
Baking time:	20 minutes
Cooling time:	20 minutes
Chilling time:	30 minutes

Preparation:

Preheat oven to 350 degrees. Butter 13x9-inch glass baking dish or metal pan. Combine cake mix, peanut butter, water, and eggs in large bowl. Stir until dough forms. Press dough into prepared dish. Bake for 20 minutes, or until puffed and set. Cool cake base for 20 minutes. Melt chocolate morsels in microwave on medium-low for about 2 minutes or until just melted and smooth, stirring every 30 seconds. Spread melted chocolate over cake base. Sprinkle with cereal. Melt butterscotch morsels in microwave on low for 30 seconds or until just melted and smooth. Drizzle over chocolate cereal and cake base in pan. Using tip of knife, swirl toppings together to create marbled effect. Refrigerate for 30 minutes, or until set. Cut into squares and serve.

PHOTO: BERLINER STUDIOS

From a teenage babysitter in Halloween *to a real-life mom of two to the best-selling author of five children's books (with more on the way), Jamie Lee Curtis knows what kids like—and they love these butterscotch fudge bars. (Adults adore them, too.) A homey mix of crunchy peanut butter and melt-in-your-mouth butterscotch, drizzled with drippy hot fudge, these quick-bake bars are comfort food fit for royalty. Down-to-earth mom Jamie is, in fact, a Baroness, an honor bestowed on her when actor-director husband Christopher Guest inherited the British Barony. Bake a batch of these butterscotch fudge bars, and everybody will eat happily ever after.*

Treat yourself to Jamie's royal performance in Trading Places *(she won a British Academy Award® for the role) or her Golden Globe®-winning performance in* True Lies.

KRISTIN DAVIS' SAVVY-SIMPLE LIMEWHIP ANGEL FOOD

Serves 6 to 8

1	purchased (12-ounce) angel food cake
1	cup boiling water
1	box (3-ounce) lime gelatin dessert mix, *Jell-O®*
1	cup cold whole milk
1	box (3.4-ounce) cheesecake-flavored instant pudding and pie filling mix, *Jell-O®*
3	tablespoons lime juice, *ReaLime®*
1 1/2	cups frozen whipped topping, thawed, *Cool Whip®* Fresh mint sprigs (optional)

Prep time:	10 minutes
Cooling time:	15 minutes
Chilling time:	1 hour

Preparation:

Place angel food cake on serving platter. Using wooden or metal skewer, pierce 3-inch-deep holes all over top of cake. Combine 1 cup of boiling water and lime gelatin mix in large bowl; stir until gelatin dissolves. Cool slightly (do not add cold water). Carefully pour 1/4 cup of warm dissolved gelatin over cake, allowing it to sink into holes. Refrigerate cake. Add milk and instant pudding mix to remaining dissolved gelatin in bowl. Whisk until smooth; whisk in lime juice. Refrigerate for 30 minutes, or until lime mixture thickens to pudding consistency. Using large rubber spatula, fold whipped topping into lime mixture. Refrigerate lime whip for 30 minutes. Spread lime whip all over cake. Refrigerate until ready to serve. Garnish with mint sprigs (optional).

Note: This cake is best eaten within 3 days.

PHOTO: MARK LIDDELL

On HBO's Sex and the City, Kristin Davis is known as the "sweet" one. Savvy on the show, she's equally savvy with a spatula. She grew up in the south where baking is highly regarded as art, and her baking skills are definitely appreciated on the set. Like Kristin—and her TV alter ego Charlotte—this simply divine angel food cake is the epitome of cool elegance. Add a halo of fresh mint, and it's positively heaven sent.

Spend a fun night with Kristin on HBO's Sex and the City.

ANTHONY EDWARDS' SUPERDAD BANANA NUT SANDWICHES

Makes 6 large or 24 bite-size sandwiches

1/2	cup chopped walnuts, toasted
2	boxes (13.9 ounces each) banana quick bread mix, *Betty Crocker®*
1 1/2	cups water
4	eggs
1/3	cup vegetable oil
3/4	cup cream cheese frosting, *Betty Crocker Rich & Creamy®*

Special equipment:
One 46-ounce can (such as from *Dole®* pineapple juice), cleaned, dried, and with 1 end of can removed

Prep time:	10 minutes
Baking time:	1 hour
Cooling time:	30 minutes
Frosting time:	10 minutes

Preparation:

Position rack in lower third of oven to allow enough space for can. Preheat oven to 350 degrees. Generously butter inside of can. Toss walnuts with 1 tablespoon of banana bread mix in small bowl to coat. Combine remaining bread mix, water, eggs, and oil in large bowl. Beat for 2 minutes, or until well blended. Stir in walnut mixture. Transfer batter to prepared can. Bake for 1 hour, or until skewer inserted into center of bread comes out clean. Cool bread in pan on cooling rack for 20 minutes. Run knife around can sides to loosen cake; invert bread onto cooling rack. Cool bread completely. Cut bread crosswise into twelve 1/2-inch-thick slices. Spread 1 tablespoon of frosting over 1 bread slice. Top with another bread slice. Repeat with remaining frosting and bread slices. Serve sandwiches whole or cut each sandwich into 4 wedges to make 24 bite-size sandwiches. Arrange sandwiches on serving platter.

Variation: Coarsely mash two fresh, ripe bananas into the cream cheese frosting for a satisfying filling.

PHOTO: BERLINER STUDIOS

Balanced meals—and a balanced life—get top billing at the Edwards' house, where Superdad Anthony puts parenting on the front burner. While wife Jeanine Lobell, founder and chairman of Stila Cosmetics, keeps stars such as Nicole Kidman, Cameron Diaz, and Julianne Moore looking beautiful, Anthony keeps their own brood of three happy with nutritious noshes, like these clever little cream cheese-filled sandwiches. They're baked in an aluminum juice can—busy dads and moms: Simply slice, fill, and serve.

Miss Anthony on E.R.*? Rent his latest film* Northfork *or travel back in time to catch his not-to-be-missed roles in* Top Gun *and* Fast Times at Ridgemont High *(Anthony's film debut).*

JULIE HAGERTY'S PERFECT POUND CAKE TRIFLE

Serves 8 to 10

1	frozen pound cake (10.75-ounce), thawed, *Sara Lee®*
1/2	cup cream sherry, *Harvey's Bristol Cream®*
2	bags (12 ounces each) frozen mixed berries, thawed and well drained
3	cups cold whole milk
1	box (5.1-ounce) vanilla instant pudding and pie filling mix, *Jell-O®*
1	container (12-ounce) frozen whipped topping, thawed, *Cool Whip®*

Prep time:	15 minutes
Chilling time:	15 minutes

Preparation:

Trim crusts off pound cake and cut cake crosswise into 3/4-inch-thick slices. Cut each cake slice diagonally in half, forming triangles. Place pound cake triangles in bottom of 2 1/2-quart clear glass bowl. Brush pound cake generously with sherry. Spoon mixed berries evenly over cake. Whisk milk and pudding mix in large bowl for 2 minutes, or until creamy and beginning to thicken. Refrigerate pudding for 5 minutes, or until pudding thickens. Pour pudding over mixed berries. Refrigerate trifle for 10 minutes. Spread whipped topping over trifle. Cover with plastic wrap and refrigerate until ready to serve.

Note: This dessert tastes even better when served the next day.

PHOTO: MIKEL HEALEY

A flighty flight attendant in Airplane!*, a yuppie dropout in* Lost in America *and a dysfunctional shrink's wife in* What About Bob?*, Julie Hagerty is not an actress to be trifled with. On-screen or on-stage, Juilliard-trained Julie's roles are always memorable — much like this pretty pound cake trifle. Triangles of rich, buttery pound cake are delectably doused in sweet sherry and layered in a glass bowl with mixed berries, pudding and whipped topping, then chilled to crowd pleasing perfection. In spring or summer, swap orange or pineapple juice for the sherry for a cool and creamy tropical treat.*

Watch Julie shine on Broadway (she's received both the Drama Critics Award and the Theatre World Award) or view her latest venture on the silver screen in A Guy Thing.

HELPFUL HINTS, TIPS, AND TRICKS

Packaging items for sale: Your local grocery store has many packaging ideas for your bake sale items. Disposable foil baking pans, especially the mini-loaf pans, are great. You can also use the decorative disposable plastic containers. Another attractive alternative: Buy inexpensive cake pans at your local discount store. You can sell the items right in the pans!

More packaging ideas: Wrap items in clear cellophane rather than plastic wrap for a more professional look. Tie packages with raffia or make your own ribbon by cutting inexpensive fabric with pinking shears.

Signs, labels, and tags: Use pinking shears or other decorating scissors to cut out signs, labels, or price tags for your baked items. Use a hole punch and a piece of raffia or ribbon to attach tags to your items. For a very natural, homegrown look, use brown butcher paper and twine.

Note: Please read each and every chapter opener as there are numerous helpful hints, tips, and tricks to know for fast, fabulous results when making a delicious *Semi-Homemade*® dessert.

for the bake sale

CHERRY LOLLIPOPS

These hard candy lollipops are the perfect project for pint-sized chefs. Make them in any color or flavor you want—even in fun shapes, using metal cookie cutters or candy molds, available at most kitchen stores. To make cute gifts, holiday treats, or party favors, tie colorful ribbons around the sticks and curl the ends by pulling the ribbons between your thumb and the blade of a pair of scissors.

Makes 20 lollipops

	Nonstick cooking spray, *PAM®*
3/4	cup granulated sugar
1/2	cup light corn syrup, *Karo®*
1/4	cup butter
1	box (3-ounce) cherry gelatin dessert mix, *Jell-O®*

Special Equipment:
20 4-inch lollipop sticks
Metal tablespoon-size measuring spoon
Candy thermometer

Prep time: 10 minutes

Preparation:

Spray 2 large baking sheets with nonstick spray.
Arrange 10 lollipop sticks on each baking sheet, spacing evenly apart.
Stir sugar, corn syrup, and butter in small saucepan over low heat until sugar has dissolved.
Slowly bring to boil, stirring frequently.
Continue cooking for 7 minutes, or until candy thermometer registers 275 degrees.
Stir in gelatin until smooth.
Using metal tablespoon and working quickly, spoon syrup over one end of each lollipop stick.
Cool completely.
Wrap each lollipop in plastic wrap and store in airtight container.

HOBO S'MORES

Hobos big and small will go coco-loco over these deliciously dippable S'Mores on a stick. Dunk them in warm chocolate, then roll in nuts, granola, fruit, or candy sprinkles for a slam dunk of a snack.

Makes 36

36	large marshmallows, *Kraft Jet-Puffed®*
1	container (16-ounce) dark chocolate frosting, *Betty Crocker Rich & Creamy®*
1 1/2	cups graham cracker crumbs, *Nabisco Honey Maid®*
1 1/2	cups semi-sweet chocolate mini morsels, *Nestlé®*

Special Equipment:
36 lollipop sticks or popsicle sticks

Prep time: 30 minutes

Preparation:

Line cookie sheet with wax paper.
Insert lollipop stick into 1 end of each marshmallow.
Microwave frosting for 30 seconds, or just until frosting feels warm to touch.
Dip 1 marshmallow at a time into frosting, allowing excess to drip off.
Dip half of marshmallow and bottom of marshmallow into graham cracker crumbs.
Dip opposite half into mini morsels.
Stand flat end down on prepared cookie sheet.
Serve immediately or refrigerate for 1 hour.

FRUIT PIZZA PIE

Turn your kitchen into a pizzeria with a piece of creative cookery the whole gang will enjoy. Easy make-and-bake pizza pies make a scrumptious snack for a birthday party, family night or weekend get-together. Set up a topping bar, pat out cookie-dough crusts, then let the kids top their own personal pizza with their favorite fruit toppings.

Serves 8 to 10

1	container (18-ounce) refrigerated sugar cookie dough, *Pillsbury®*
1	container (8-ounce) cream cheese, *Philadelphia®*
2	tablespoons granulated sugar
1	teaspoon pure vanilla extract, *McCormick®*
1/4	cup seedless red raspberry jam
2	kiwi fruit, peeled, sliced
3	canned peaches, drained, patted dry, thinly sliced, *Del Monte®*
1/4	cup fresh raspberries or blueberries
2	tablespoons sweetened flaked coconut, toasted, *Baker's®*

Prep time:	10 minutes
Baking time:	20 minutes
Cooling time:	45 minutes

Preparation:

Preheat oven to 375 degrees.

Roll cookie dough into ball, then press into shallow round pizza pan or 9-inch-diameter cake pan.

Bake for 20 minutes, or until golden brown.

Cool crust completely in pan on cooling rack.

Combine cream cheese, sugar, and vanilla in large bowl.

Beat for 3 minutes, or until light and fluffy.

Spread cream cheese mixture over crust.

Spread jam over cream cheese.

Decorate with kiwi slices, peaches, raspberries, and toasted coconut.

Chocolate Lover's Pizza Variation: Make crust with roll of refrigerated chocolate chip cookie dough. Top with hot fudge topping, mini marshmallows, chocolate morsels, and toasted slivered almonds. Rewarm pizza in oven until marshmallows begin to melt.

Variation: White frosting can be substituted for cream cheese.

CINNAMON SUGAR CRUMBLE CAKES

Makes 3 small loaves

	Nonstick cooking spray, *PAM®*
1/4	cup instant coffee granules, *Maxwell House®*
2	tablespoons hot water
1	box (21-ounce) cinnamon crumb cake mix, *Krusteaz®*
1/2	cup water
1	egg, beaten to blend
2	6-inch biscotti cookies, crushed

Special Equipment:
Three 5 3/4x3 1/4x2-inch disposable miniature loaf pans

Prep time:	10 minutes
Cooking time:	35 minutes

Preparation:

Preheat oven to 350 degrees.

Spray loaf pans with nonstick spray.

Stir coffee granules and 2 tablespoons of hot water in large bowl until granules dissolve.

Add cake mix packet, 1/2 cup of water, and egg.

Stir just until moistened (mixture will be lumpy).

Stir topping mixture and crushed biscotti in medium bowl.

Spoon half of topping mixture into prepared loaf pans.

Spoon batter over topping mixture.

Spoon remaining topping mixture atop batter.

Bake for 35 minutes, or until toothpick inserted into center of loaves comes out clean.

Serve warm or at room temperature.

DOUBLE DECKER FUDGE

Makes 36 pieces

4	cups semi-sweet chocolate morsels, *Nestlé®*
2	cans (14 ounces each) sweetened condensed milk, *Carnation®*
2	teaspoons pure vanilla extract, *McCormick®*
3	cups premier white morsels, *Nestlé®*

Prep time: 30 minutes, chilling time: 3 hours

Preparation:

Line 8-inch-square glass or metal baking pan with foil, allowing 2 inches of foil to hang over sides. Combine 3 1/2 cups of semi-sweet morsels, 2 cups of condensed milk, and vanilla in large glass bowl. Heat in microwave on medium power for 1 1/2 minutes, stirring every 30 seconds, or until melted and smooth. Pour half of semi-sweet chocolate fudge into prepared pan; smooth top with spatula. Immediately sprinkle 1/4 cup of white morsels over fudge. Let stand 30 seconds for morsels to melt slightly. Using toothpick or wooden skewer, swirl chocolates together to form marbled effect. Combine 2 1/2 cups of white morsels and remaining condensed milk in medium glass bowl. Heat in microwave on medium power for 2 minutes, stirring every 30 seconds, or until melted and smooth. Pour white fudge atop semi-sweet chocolate fudge in pan; smooth top with spatula. Immediately sprinkle remaining 1/2 cup of semi-sweet morsels over fudge. Let stand 30 seconds for morsels to melt slightly. Using toothpick or wooden skewer, swirl chocolates together to form marbled effect. Pour remaining warm semi-sweet chocolate fudge atop white fudge in pan; smooth top with spatula. Immediately sprinkle remaining 1/4 cup of white morsels over fudge. Refrigerate for at least 3 hours, or until fudge is firm. Peel away foil and cut fudge into squares or desired shapes.

CARAMEL POPCORN CONES

Makes twelve 2-inch popcorn balls

18	soft caramel candies, unwrapped, *Brach's Milk Maid®*
2	tablespoons whole milk
1/2	cup finely chopped walnuts, toasted
1	package (3-ounce) microwave popcorn, popped, or about 4 cups popped popcorn, *Orville Redenbacher's®*

Prep time: 20 minutes

Preparation:

Line cookie sheet with wax paper. Melt caramels with milk in microwave on low heat for 1 1/2 minutes, stirring every 30 seconds, or until smooth. Stir walnuts into caramel. Using about 1/3 cup of popcorn for each ball, dip one end of each popcorn kernel into melted caramel and adhere to another popcorn kernel. Repeat with remaining popcorn, forming twelve 2-inch-diameter popcorn balls. Store in airtight container at room temperature.

for the bake sale

NUTTY BRITTLE

Makes 30 servings

	Nonstick cooking spray, *PAM®*
24	soft caramel candies, unwrapped, *Brach's Milk Maid®*
3/4	cup toffee peanuts

Prep time:	15 minutes
Chilling time:	30 minutes

Preparation:

Preheat oven to 200 degrees. Line jelly roll pan with foil. Spray foil with cooking spray and place in warm oven. Spray heavy small saucepan with cooking spray. Add caramels and stir over low heat until melted. Stir in toffee peanuts and continue stirring for 5 minutes. Quickly spread caramel-peanut mixture over prepared pan. Cool completely. Cover pan with plastic and refrigerate for 30 minutes. Break into bite-size pieces. Store in refrigerator.

RICE CRISPY PEANUT BUTTER TREATS

Makes 36

3	cups rice cereal, *Kellogg's®*
1	cup extra crunchy peanut butter, *Jif®*
1	cup peanut butter chips, *Reese's®*
1	jar (7-ounce) marshmallow creme, *Kraft Jet-Puffed®*

Prep time:	5 minutes
Chilling time:	1 hour

Preparation:

Line cookie sheet with wax paper. Using 2 wooden spoons, toss rice cereal, peanut butter and peanut butter chips in large bowl to coat. Add marshmallow creme and toss until well combined. Using 1-ounce cookie scoop, form mixture into 1 1/2-inch balls. Place on prepared cookie sheet. Refrigerate for 1 hour, or until firm. Store in airtight container.

OATMEAL DATE SPICE COOKIES

These comfort cookies are so homey they're like a food hug. I bake a big batch whenever I need a quick pick-me-up. They take only 15 minutes and are perfect for a picnic or a no-guilt grab-'n'-go snack. If you don't want to use dates, substitute the same amount of raisins, currants, or dried cranberries. Or bake all four, so you'll never run out.

Makes about 36 cookies

1	box (18.25-ounce) classic yellow cake mix, *Duncan Hines Moist Deluxe®*
1 1/2	sticks butter, melted
1/3	cup all purpose flour
2	eggs
2	tablespoons pumpkin pie spice, *McCormick®*
2	teaspoons pure vanilla extract, *McCormick®*
1	cup quick-cooking oats, *Quaker Oats®*
1	cup walnuts, chopped, toasted
1	cup chopped dates, *Sunsweet®*

Prep time:	5 minutes
Baking time:	10 minutes
Cooling time:	5 minutes

Preparation:

Preheat oven to 375 degrees.
Combine cake mix, melted butter, flour, eggs, pumpkin pie spice, and vanilla in large bowl.
Beat for 1 minute, or until well blended.
Stir in oats, walnuts, and dates.
Drop heaping tablespoons of dough onto ungreased cookie sheet, spacing 2 inches apart.
Cook for 10 minutes, or until edges begin to brown.
Cool cookies on cookie sheet for 5 minutes.
Transfer cookies to cooling rack or platter.

Note: To save a lot of time and effort, always buy pre-chopped dates. If you need to chop your own, spray your knife or the blades of your food processor with nonstick cooking spray to minimize sticking.

For the Romantic

HELPFUL HINTS, TIPS, AND TRICKS

Create a Romantic Mood: Park phones and pagers at the door and create an intimate sanctuary with no intrusions. Surround yourself with simple luxuries—a snuggly blanket, a bowl of chocolate-covered cherries (see p. 111), or sensuous chocolate truffles (see p. 115).

Feel Soft and Sexy: Slip into something strokable, like sleek satin or cuddly cashmere. For sensually kiss-me-quick lips (see p. 119), think pink. Put romance in the air with a spritz of champagne perfume (p. 116).

Play Seductive Music: Set the stage for an amorous evening with music that's as smooth as champagne. Relaxing to *Sade, "Love Deluxe"* helps you unwind; *John Coltrane, "Coltrane for Lovers"* jazzes things up.

Light Candles and Display Flowers: A wash of softly scented candlelight stimulates desire—try woodsy patchouli or sweet gardenia. Colors and flowers invite romance—red roses spell true love; purple orchids kindle passion.

S T R A W B E R R Y   T U X E D O   C A K E

Serves 10 to 12

1	box (18.25-ounce) classic white cake mix, *Duncan Hines Moist Deluxe®*
1 1/3	cups water
3	eggs
2	tablespoons vegetable oil
3/4	cup strawberry jam
1	container (16-ounce) classic vanilla frosting, *Duncan Hines Creamy Home-Style®*
1/4	cup semi-sweet chocolate mini-morsels, melted, *Nestlé®*

Special Ingredients:
3/4 cup ready-to-use pure white rolled fondant, *Wilton®*
10-12 purchased tuxedo strawberries or chocolate-dipped strawberries

Prep time: 10 minutes, bake time: 20 minutes, cooling time: 30 minutes
Chilling time: 30 minutes, decorating time: 25 minutes

P r e p a r a t i o n :

Preheat oven to 350 degrees. Butter and flour four 8-inch-diameter round cake pans. Combine cake mix, water, eggs, and oil in large bowl. Beat for 2 minutes, or until well blended. Divide batter among prepared pans. Bake for 20 minutes, or until toothpick inserted into center of cakes comes out clean. Cool cakes in pans on cooling racks for 15 minutes. Invert cakes onto cooling racks and cool completely. Spread 1/4 cup of jam over the top of each of three cakes. Place cake layers atop each other on serving platter, ending with plain cake layer. Spread frosting smoothly over top and sides of cake to coat completely. Refrigerate for 30 minutes.

TO DECORATE: Roll out 1/4 cup of fondant into thin 10-inch-long log. Cut log crosswise into small pieces and roll into pea-sized balls. Gently flatten each ball into button shape. Roll out remaining 1/2 cup of fondant between 2 sheets of plastic into 1/8-inch thickness. Cut out 1-inch squares. Cut each square diagonally in half to form triangles. Using fork, draw lines through chilled frosting to resemble pleats. Gently press fondant triangles into frosting around top edge of cake to resemble bow ties. Gently press fondant buttons below bow ties into frosting. Press chocolate morsels into center of bow ties. Garnish with tuxedo strawberries or chocolate-dipped strawberries.

Variation: To make 3-4 smaller cakes for single servings, divide the batter into 3-4 equal portions and bake in miniature cake pans (approximately 3 inches round). Frost and decorate as instructed and serve on individual cake pedestals or dessert plates.

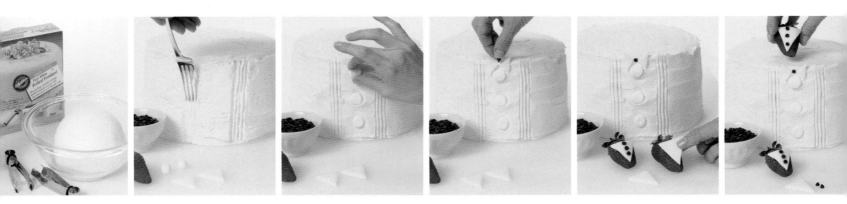

CHOCOLATE-COVERED CHERRIES

These chocolate-covered cherries are absolutely addictive. For a fun yet elegant dessert, pour a splash of cherry syrup into a martini glass, then top off with white- and dark-dipped cherries. For a more spirited dessert, spike the syrup with brandy or a fruit liqueur, like Grand Marnier®. Eat the cherries, then drink the syrup for a nightcap chaser. To add black tie style to a dinner party or buffet, group filled glasses on stacked silver trays and have them do double duty as a centerpiece, or set a filled glass at each place setting to complete your tablescape. To make thoughtful gifts for anniversaries and other red letter days, fill a red takeout container and give that special someone a box of bonbons.

Makes 40

40	maraschino cherries with stems (packed in heavy syrup), drained well
1/2	cup (3 ounces) semi-sweet chocolate morsels, *Nestlé®*
1/2	cup (3 ounces) premier white morsels, *Nestlé®*

Prep time:	20 minutes
Chilling time:	40 minutes

Preparation:

Line cookie sheet with parchment paper or wax paper.

Pat cherries dry with paper towels.

Melt chocolates separately in stainless steel bowl set over pan of simmering water, stirring until smooth.

Holding stem of cherry, dip cherry into melted chocolate to coat.

Transfer chocolate-dipped cherry to prepared cookie sheet.

Repeat with remaining cherries and melted chocolate.

Refrigerate for about 40 minutes, or until set.

CHOCOLATE BOX WITH
EASY CHOCOLATE MOUSSE

Serves 2

1	cup frozen whipped topping, thawed, *Cool Whip*®
2	containers (3.5 ounces each) prepared chocolate-flavored pudding, *Kraft Handi Snack*®
3	chocolate bars (4.5 ounces each), milk chocolate, or bittersweet chocolate
1	container chocolate frosting, *Pillsbury Creamy Supreme*®
	Fresh raspberries

Prep time:	15 minutes
Chilling time:	20 minutes

Special Equipment:
Pastry bag
Large star tip

Preparation:

Combine whipped topping and pudding in large bowl.
Using rubber spatula, fold just until blended.
Refrigerate chocolate mousse until ready to serve.
Cut chocolate bars crosswise in half.
Adhere sides together with chocolate frosting to form box.
Refrigerate until firm.
Pipe chocolate mousse into chilled chocolate box.
Top with raspberries and serve.

Note: The chocolate mousse is also delicious on its own. Serve it in large wine goblets, and garnish with whipped topping and raspberries for an elegant presentation.

SENSUOUS CHOCOLATE TRUFFLES

In France, chocolate truffles are more than dessert; they're a national pastime. It's easy to see why, especially when the truffles are as sinfully chocolatey as these. Don't worry about shaping them into precise balls—it's the little peaks that give them charm. Truffles freeze beautifully, so make several batches and store them in the freezer for impromptu gifts, drop-by guests or spur-of-the-moment gatherings. To celebrate holidays or birthdays with sweet style, mix truffles with cookies or candy on a dessert tray or in a gift box. You'll make someone—or lots of someones—very happy.

Makes about 36 truffles

1	container (16-ounce) chocolate frosting, *Betty Crocker Rich & Creamy®*
3/4	cup confectioners/powdered sugar, sifted
1	teaspoon pure vanilla extract, *McCormick®*
1/2	cup unsweetened cocoa powder, *Hershey's®*

Prep time:	15 minutes
Chilling time:	1 hour

Preparation:

Line 2 cookie sheets with parchment paper.

Beat frosting, confectioners/powdered sugar, and vanilla in large bowl until smooth.

Using tablespoon or 1-ounce cookie scoop, form mixture into balls and place on cookie sheet.

Dust truffles with cocoa powder.

Cover and refrigerate truffles until ready to serve.

ALTERNATIVE TRUFFLE FLAVORS:

Instead of dusting the truffles with cocoa powder, chill them until slightly firm, then dip them in:

Chocolate sprinkles, chopped nuts, toasted coconut, or semi-sweet chocolate mini morsels.

Instead of dusting the truffles with cocoa powder, chill them until slightly firm, then dip them in:

Melted semi-sweet chocolate or white chocolate, and roll them in chopped nuts.

Substitute the vanilla extract with:

Orange, rum, peppermint, or almond extract.

Form the truffle mixture around the following before dusting, rolling or dipping:
Hershey's Kisses® or *Hershey's Kisses with Almonds®*, small *Reese's Peanut Butter Cups®*, or well-drained maraschino cherries.

for the romantic

CHAMPAGNE PERFUME

There's nothing like champagne to add sparkle to an evening. Now you can drink your bubbly and wear it, too. Just swirl a little rose water into a glass of pink champagne for a spirited spritzer that'll have you feeling in the pink. Fill an atomizer and tuck it in the nightstand for those times you want to be absolutely intoxicating.

Makes about 1/2 cup

1/2	cup pink champagne, *Andre*®
1/4	cup rose flower water, *Indo-European*®

Prep time:	5 minutes
Chilling time:	1 day

Preparation:

Stir champagne and rose flower water in 1-cup measuring cup.
Cover and refrigerate until bubbles disappear, stirring occasionally, about 1 day.
Transfer to your favorite perfume bottle.
Keep refrigerated.

Note: Rose flower water can be found in the ethnic foods section or liquor department of most grocery stores, or at drug stores.

PINK LINEN DUSTING POWDER

He always said you're sweet as sugar. Show him how right he is with this pearly pink powder that shimmers sweetly in the light. It's as quietly come-hither as fairy dust and every bit as enchanting. Dust lightly across your shoulders and chest and down your back and arms. Don't forget your cleavage! Sensational for a special night out…or a special night in.

Makes about 1/4 cup

2	tablespoons confectioners/powdered sugar
10	red Wonka Pixy Stix candies, *Nestlé*®

Prep time: 5 minutes

Preparation:

Stir confectioners/powdered sugar and contents of Pixy Stix into small bowl to blend.
Sift mixture into another small bowl.
Repeat until dusting powder is evenly colored.
Apply to yourself or friend with new makeup brush or powder puff.

LIP GLOSS

Makes about 1/4 cup

2	tablespoons cherry or blueberry preserves, *Smucker's®*
1	tablespoon vegetable oil
1	teaspoon light corn syrup, *Karo®*
1/2	teaspoon imitation cherry extract, *McCormick®*

Prep time: 5 minutes, cooling time: 30 minutes

Preparation:

Whisk all ingredients in heavy small saucepan over low heat until beginning to boil. Strain mixture through sieve into small bowl. Cool mixture completely, stirring occasionally. Using spatula, transfer lip gloss to decorative container. Cover and refrigerate.

KISS ME LIP BALM

Makes about 1/3 cup

1/2	cup confectioners/powdered sugar
1/4	cup solid vegetable shortening, *Crisco®*
	Food coloring (color optional)
1	teaspoon pure peppermint extract, *McCormick®*

Prep time: 5 minutes

Preparation:

Beat confectioners/powdered sugar and shortening in medium bowl for 2 minutes or until smooth. Mix in food coloring, 1 drop at a time, until desired color is achieved. Mix in peppermint extract. Using spatula, transfer lip balm to decorative container. Cover and keep at room temperature.

BODY PAINT

Makes about 2 cups

1	container (12-ounce) fluffy white frosting, *Betty Crocker Whipped®*
6	tablespoons light corn syrup, *Karo®*
	Assorted food colorings
	Assorted flavor extracts: lemon, orange, almond, peppermint, vanilla, *McCormick®*

Prep time: 5 minutes

Preparation:

Mix frosting and syrup in medium bowl until smooth. Divide mixture into 3 small bowls. Add 1 drop of each food coloring to each bowl. Mix and match colors and flavors as desired. Apply with clean pastry brush or new small paint brush.

SUGGESTED COLOR AND FLAVOR PAIRINGS:
Yellow food coloring with 1/4 teaspoon lemon extract
Red and yellow food coloring with 1/4 teaspoon orange extract
Green food coloring with 1/2 teaspoon almond extract
Red food coloring with 1/4 teaspoon peppermint extract
Blue food coloring with 1/2 teaspoon vanilla extract

For the Special Occasion

HELPFUL HINTS, TIPS, AND TRICKS

Parchment paper: Parchment paper is a grease- and moisture-resistant paper with many culinary virtues. You can make disposable pastry bags or line baking sheets for even cooking.

Latex gloves: These disposable gloves can be purchased in most grocery stores or shops that specialize in cake decorating.

Fondant: We bought ready-to-use rolled fondant. It is easy to work with and comes with step-by-step directions enclosed in the box. You can color white fondant any color. Drop the dye onto fondant a drop at a time, kneading the fondant until the desired color is achieved. It is best to wear disposable latex gloves to keep the color from staining your hands.

Coloring marzipan: Color marzipan by kneading in liquid food coloring drop by drop. It is best to wear disposable latex gloves to keep the color from staining your hands.

Note: Please read each and every chapter opener as there are numerous helpful hints, tips, and tricks to know for fast, fabulous results when making a delicious *Semi-Homemade®* dessert.

PINK MERINGUE KISSES

Makes 24

3	egg whites, at room temperature
1/4	teaspoon cream of tartar, *McCormick®*
3/4	cup granulated sugar
1	teaspoon imitation strawberry extract, *McCormick®*
3	drops red food coloring

Special Equipment:
Pastry bag
#4 star tip

Prep time:	15 minutes
Baking time:	3 hours
Cooling time:	20 minutes

Preparation:

Preheat oven to 200 degrees. Line 2 heavy large baking sheets with parchment paper. Beat egg whites in clean large metal bowl on medium speed until foamy. Add cream of tartar. Increase speed to high and continue beating until soft peaks form. Gradually add sugar, 1 tablespoon at a time, beating until stiff peaks form, about 5 minutes. Quickly mix in strawberry extract. Stir in food coloring, 1 drop at a time, until desired color is achieved. Spoon meringue into pastry bag fitted with star tip. Pipe twelve 1 1/2-inch-high by 1 1/2-inch-diameter mounds onto each prepared baking sheet, spacing evenly apart. Bake for 3 hours, or until dry and crisp. Cool meringues completely on baking sheets. Store in airtight container at room temperature.

White Meringues Variation: Omit the red food coloring and use 1 teaspoon of white vanilla or 1/2 teaspoon of white crème de cacao instead of the strawberry extract.

Mint Meringues Variation: Substitute 1/2 teaspoon of mint extract or white crème de menthe and 2-3 drops of green food coloring, adding slowly until the meringues are pale green.

Note: To ensure a completely smooth meringue the sugar must be added a tablespoon at a time. When making meringues, it is very important to have any equipment (bowls, mixers, spatulas, spoons) scrupulously clean. Any grease or fat can wreck an egg-white foam. If your meringues keep breaking, fat or grease could be the cause. Rub equipment with lemon juice, then rinse and dry completely to get rid of all traces of fat. Humidity is always a factor when making meringues. An old adage states never to make meringues on a damp day. It's true: When the sugar in meringues absorbs moisture it turns soft and sticky.

PASTEL PETIT FOURS

Makes 12

CAKE:

1	frozen pound cake (16-ounce), thawed, *Sara Lee®*
1/3	cup plus 2 tablespoons seedless red raspberry jam
1	tablespoon water

FONDANT DECORATIONS:

	Assorted food colorings (colors optional)
	Confectioners/powdered sugar
1/2	cup fluffy white frosting, *Betty Crocker Whipped®*
12	sugar-coated jelly candies

Special Equipment and Ingredients:
Disposable latex gloves; 1/2 box (24-ounce) ready-to-use pure white rolled fondant, *Wilton®*; pastry bag; small star tip

Prep time: 50 minutes

Preparation:

Using sharp knife, trim crust from cake. Cut cake crosswise into six 1 1/2-inch-thick slices. Cut each slice vertically in half to make 12 pieces. Trim any uneven sides with sharp knife. Slice each cake in half and spread 1/2 teaspoon of jam over 6 pieces. Top with remaining cake pieces and set aside. Whisk 1/3 cup of jam and water in small bowl until smooth to make glaze. Brush raspberry glaze over tops and sides of cakes.

FOR THE FONDANT: Divide fondant into 6 pieces. Wearing gloves, knead 1 food coloring, 1 drop at a time, into each fondant piece until desired color is achieved. Divide each colored fondant in half. Sprinkle work surface and rolling pin with confectioners/powdered sugar. Roll out 1 fondant piece at a time into 5-inch diameter that is 1/4 inch thick, rotating to prevent sticking. Drape fondant over 1 prepared cake; smooth over surface. Trim excess fondant from around base of cake. Repeat with remaining cakes and fondant pieces. Spoon frosting into pastry bag fitted with star tip. Pipe frosting atop cakes. Decorate with candies. Store in airtight container.

Variation: Use cookie cutters to cut cake slices into desired shapes.

TWO-TIER LEMON YELLOW CAKE WITH SUGARED ROSES

Serves 30 to 40

3	boxes (18.25 ounces each) lemon cake mix, *Betty Crocker SuperMoist*®
3 3/4	cups water
9	eggs
1	cup vegetable oil
1 1/3	cups lemon curd, stirred to loosen
3	containers (12 ounces each) fluffy white or lemon frosting, *Betty Crocker Whipped*®

Special Equipment and Ingredients:
One 10-inch-diameter round cake pan with 3-inch-high sides; one 7-inch-diameter round cake pan with 3-inch-high sides; two cardboard cake rounds (one 10-inch and one 7-inch); two 12 3/8-inch-long, 3/8-inch-diameter plastic dowel rods, *Wilton*®; edible sugared roses or silk fabric roses

Prep time: 30 minutes, baking time: 1 1/2 hours, cooling time: 1 hour
Decorating time: 25 minutes

Cake Preparation:

Preheat oven to 350 degrees. Butter and flour cake pans. Combine 2 cake mixes, 2 1/2 cups of water, 6 eggs, and 2/3 cup of oil in large bowl. Beat for 3 minutes, or until well blended. Transfer batter to 10-inch cake pan. Combine 1 cake mix, 1 1/4 cups of water, 3 eggs, and 1/3 cup of oil in same bowl. Beat for 2 minutes, or until well blended. Transfer batter to 7-inch cake pan. Bake 10-inch cake for 1 1/2 hours and 7-inch cake for 1 hour, or until toothpick inserted into center of cakes comes out clean. Cool cakes in pans on cooling racks for 20 minutes. Invert cakes onto cooling racks and cool completely.

Filling and Frosting Preparations:

Cut cakes horizontally in half. Place 1 tablespoon of lemon curd in center of each cardboard round. Place 10-inch cake top, cut side up, atop 10-inch cardboard round. Spread 1 cup of curd over cake; top with 10-inch cake bottom, cut side down. Place 7-inch cake top, cut side up, atop 7-inch cardboard round. Spread 1/3 cup of curd over cake; top with 7-inch cake bottom, cut side down. Spread thin layer of frosting over cakes. Refrigerate until cold. Spread remaining frosting over cakes to coat completely. Using toothpick, swirl frosting decoratively.

To Assemble:

Cut dowel rods crosswise into five 3-inch-long pieces. Place 10-inch cake on platter. Press 4 cut rods into cake, positioning about 3 1/2 inches in from edge and spacing evenly. Press 1 rod into center. Place 7-inch cake on cardboard atop rods in 10-inch cake. Place sugared or silk roses over cakes before serving.

DOUBLE CHOCOLATE CAKE WITH CHOCOLATE LEAVES

Serves 18

CAKE AND FROSTING:

1	box (18.25-ounce) devil's food cake mix, *Duncan Hines Moist Deluxe®*
1 1/3	cups water
1/2	cup vegetable oil
3	eggs
2	containers (16 ounces each) dark chocolate frosting, *Betty Crocker Rich & Creamy®*

CHOCOLATE LEAVES:

1/2	cup semi-sweet chocolate morsels, *Nestlé®*
1/2	cup milk chocolate morsels, *Nestlé®*

Special equipment:
One 9-inch-diameter round cake pan with 3-inch-high sides
One 6-inch-diameter round cake pan with 3-inch-high sides
Twenty lemon leaves, washed and dried well

Prep time: 25 minutes, baking time: 35 minutes, cooling time: 1 hour
Chilling time: 20 minutes, decorating time: 25 minutes

Preparation:

Preheat oven to 350 degrees. Butter and flour cake pans. Combine cake mix, water, oil, and eggs in large bowl. Beat for 3 minutes, or until well blended. Divide batter proportionately between prepared pans. Bake for 35 minutes, or until toothpick inserted into center of cakes comes out clean. Cool cakes in pans on cooling racks for 15 minutes. Invert cakes onto cooling racks and cool completely.

FOR THE FROSTING:

Slice each cake horizontally in half. Place 9-inch cake top, cut side up, on serving platter. Spread 1/2 cup of frosting over cake; top with 9-inch cake bottom, cut side down. Place 6-inch cake top, cut side up, on work surface. Spread 1/4 cup of frosting over cake; top with 6-inch cake bottom, cut side down. Frost cakes with remaining frosting. Refrigerate for 20 minutes.

FOR THE CHOCOLATE LEAVES:

Line cookie sheet with parchment or wax paper. Melt each kind of chocolate separately in microwave for 1 1/2 minutes, stirring every 30 seconds, or until smooth. Using offset spatula, spread underside of leaves with melted chocolates. Place leaves, chocolate side up, on prepared cookie sheet. Do not allow chocolate to drip over leaf edges. Refrigerate until set, then peel away leaf. Place 6-inch cake atop 9-inch cake. Arrange chocolate leaves decoratively atop cakes.

for the special occasion

baby shower

BABY FONDANT PACKAGES

Serves 30 to 40

CAKE:

3	boxes (18.25 ounces each) classic white cake mix, *Duncan Hines Moist Deluxe®*
4	cups water
9	egg whites
1/4	cup plus 2 tablespoons vegetable oil
2	cups apricot preserves, *Smucker's®*

FONDANT DECORATION:

Confectioners/powdered sugar
Green, pink, blue, and yellow food colorings

Special Equipment and Ingredients:
One 10-inch-square cake pan with 3-inch-high sides; one 8-inch-square cake pan with 3-inch-high sides; two cardboard cake boards (one 10-inch-square and one 8-inch-square); two boxes (24 ounces each) ready-to-use pure white rolled fondant, *Wilton®*; three pairs of disposable latex gloves; small moon- and star-shaped cookie cutters; gum arabic; baby-themed decorations

Prep time: 15 minutes, baking time: 1 hour 15 minutes, cooling time: 1 hour
Decorating time: 1 hour

Preparation:

Preheat oven to 350 degrees. Butter and flour cake pans. Combine 2 cake mixes, 2 2/3 cups of water, 6 egg whites, and 1/4 cup of oil in large bowl. Beat for 3 minutes, or until well blended. Pour batter into 10-inch pan. Combine 1 cake mix, 1 1/3 cups of water, 3 egg whites, and 2 tablespoons of oil in same bowl. Beat for 2 minutes, or until well blended. Pour batter into 8-inch pan. Bake 10-inch cake for 1 hour 15 minutes, and 8-inch cake for 55 minutes, or until toothpick inserted into center of cakes comes out clean. Cool cakes in pans on cooling racks for 30 minutes. Invert cakes onto cooling racks and cool completely. Stir preserves in heavy small saucepan over medium-high heat until beginning to boil. Strain preserves into small bowl (glaze). Spoon 1 tablespoon of glaze into center of each cardboard round. Place boards, glaze side down, atop cakes. Invert cakes onto boards. Brush remaining glaze over cakes.

FOR THE FONDANT: Sprinkle work surface and rolling pin with confectioners/powdered sugar. Wearing gloves, knead green food coloring, 1 drop at a time, into fondant from 1 box. Roll out green fondant into18-inch-square that is 1/4 inch thick, rotating to prevent sticking. Pierce bubbles that appear in fondant. Slide hands under fondant and drape over 10-inch cake; smooth over surface. Trim excess fondant from around base of cake. Brush off excess confectioners/powdered sugar. Knead trimmings together; wrap in plastic. Knead pink food coloring, 1 drop at a time, into 1/2 cup of white fondant. Knead blue food coloring, 1 drop at a time, into 1/2 cup of white fondant. Wrap pink and blue fondants separately in plastic; set aside. Knead yellow food coloring, 1 drop at a time, into remaining fondant from second box. Roll out yellow fondant into 15-inch-square that is 1/4 inch thick. Slide hands under fondant and drape over 8-inch cake; smooth over surface. Knead trimmings together; wrap in plastic. Place 8-inch cake atop 10-inch cake. Roll out colored fondant trimmings separately into 1/4-inch thickness. Cut out shapes from fondant with cookie cutters. Moisten shapes with water, then dab gum arabic onto moistened side; press shapes onto cakes to adhere.

for the special occasion
birthday

BIRTHDAY STAGE CAKE

2	boxes (18.25 ounces each) strawberry cake mix, *Pillsbury Moist Supreme®*
2 2/3	cups water
1	cup vegetable oil
6	eggs
3/4	cup strawberry jam
2	containers (12 ounces each) fluffy white, lemon, or strawberry frosting, *Betty Crocker Whipped®*

Special Equipment:
Assorted circus-themed decorations

Prep time:	20 minutes
Baking time:	40 minutes
Cooling time:	40 minutes
Decorating time:	30 minutes

Preparation:

Preheat oven to 350 degrees.

Butter and flour two 9-inch-diameter round cake pans with 2-inch-high sides.

Combine cake mixes, water, oil, and eggs in very large bowl.

Beat for 3 minutes, or until well blended.

Divide batter between prepared pans.

Bake for 40 minutes, or until toothpick inserted into center of cakes comes out clean.

Cool cakes in pans on cooling rack for 15 minutes.

Invert cakes onto cooling rack and cool completely.

Cut 1 cake horizontally in half.

Place top cake layer, cut side up, on serving platter.

Spread 1/2 cup of jam over cake layer.

Top with bottom cake layer, cut side down.

Cut second cake vertically in half, forming 2 half-circle pieces.

Spread remaining jam over top of 1 half-circle cake.

Top with second half-circle cake.

Place stacked half-circle cakes atop cake on platter.

Spread entire cake with frosting to coat completely.

Arrange purchased decorations on cake to resemble circus stage.

MOCHA CAKE WITH CHOCOLATE CROWN

Serves 12 to 16

CAKE:
1 1/3	cups hot water
1/2	cup instant coffee crystals, *Maxwell House®*
1	box (18.25-ounce) devil's food cake mix, *Duncan Hines Moist Deluxe®*
1/2	cup vegetable oil
3	eggs

FILLING AND FROSTING:
1/4	cup instant coffee crystals, *Maxwell House®*
2	tablespoons hot water
1	container (8-ounce) frozen whipped topping, thawed, *Cool Whip®*
1	container (16-ounce) classic chocolate fudge frosting, *Duncan Hines Creamy Home-Style®*

CHOCOLATE CROWN:
1	package (12-ounce) semi-sweet chocolate morsels, *Nestlé®*
1 1/2	cups premier white morsels, *Nestlé®*
	Additional semi-sweet chocolate morsels, *Nestlé®*

Prep time: 30 minutes, baking time: 35 minutes, cooling time: 45 minutes
Chilling time: 1 1/2 hours, decorating time: 30 minutes

Preparation:

Preheat oven to 350 degrees. Butter and flour two 8-inch-diameter round cake pans. Stir hot water and coffee crystals in large bowl until crystals dissolve. Add cake mix, oil, and eggs to coffee mixture. Beat for 2 minutes, or until well blended. Divide batter between prepared pans. Bake for 35 minutes, or until toothpick inserted into center of cakes comes out clean. Cool cakes in pans on cooling racks for 15 minutes. Invert cakes onto cooling racks and cool completely.

FOR THE FILLING AND FROSTING: Stir coffee crystals and hot water in medium bowl until crystals dissolve. Refrigerate for 30 minutes, or until cold. Fold whipped topping into cold coffee mixture just until blended; set mocha cream aside. Cut each cake horizontally in half. Place top cake layer, cut side up, on serving platter. Spread 1 cup of mocha cream atop cake. Top with bottom cake layer, cut side down. Spread 1 cup of mocha cream over second cake layer. Repeat layering with third cake layer and remaining mocha cream. Top with remaining bottom cake layer, cut side down. Refrigerate for 30 minutes. Spread chocolate frosting evenly over cake to cover completely. Return to refrigerator.

FOR THE CHOCOLATE CROWN: Draw three 6-inch-high crown designs over three 15-inch-long sheets of parchment paper. Cut out designs from parchment papers. Lay each crown parchment template on large baking sheet. Melt chocolate morsels in microwave for 2 1/2 minutes, stirring every 30 seconds, or until melted and smooth. Repeat with white morsels. Using offset spatula, spread melted chocolate thickly over 1 side of 2 crown templates. Repeat with melted white morsels and remaining crown template. Arrange additional chocolate morsels decoratively on white crown. Refrigerate for 30 minutes, or until chocolate is set. Wrap 1 chocolate template around half of cake; carefully peel off paper. Wrap second chocolate crown around remaining half of cake; carefully peel off paper. Seal ends of crowns with hot knife. Refrigerate cake until chocolate crown is completely firm. Wrap white crown, paper side inward, around 5-inch-diameter bowl. Refrigerate until white crown is completely firm. Carefully peel paper from white crown. Place white crown atop cake.

for the special occasion
birthday

THE PERFECT PACKAGE

Serves 30 to 35

CAKE:
3   boxes (18.25 ounces each) classic white cake mix, *Duncan Hines Moist Deluxe*®
4   cups water
9   egg whites
1/4   cup plus 2 tablespoons vegetable oil

AMARETTO FILLING:
1   package (8-ounce) cream cheese, at room temperature, *Philadelphia*®
1   stick (4-ounce) butter, at room temperature
2   tablespoons *Amaretto di Saronno*®
3 1/2   cups confectioners/powdered sugar
1   jar (16-ounce) apricot preserves, *Smucker's*®
1   tablespoon water

FONDANT DECORATION:
        Blue food coloring
        Confectioners/powdered sugar

Special Equipment and Ingredients:
Three 9-inch-square baking pans with 2 1/2-inch-high sides; disposable latex gloves; 2 boxes (24 ounces each) ready-to-use pure white rolled fondant, *Wilton*®; white ribbon (1 inch wide); gum arabic

Prep time: 35 minutes, baking time: 30 minutes, cooling time: 45 minutes
Decorating time: 25 minutes

Preparation:

Preheat oven to 350 degrees. Butter and flour cake pans. Combine cake mix, water, egg whites, and oil in very large bowl. Beat for 3 minutes, or until well blended. Divide batter among prepared pans. Bake for 30 minutes, or until toothpick inserted into center of cakes comes out clean. Cool cakes in pans on cooling racks for 15 minutes. Invert cakes onto cooling racks and cool completely.

FOR THE AMARETTO FILLING: Beat cream cheese, butter, and Amaretto in large bowl until smooth. Gradually beat in confectioners/powdered sugar. Place 1 cake layer on serving platter. Spread half of filling over top of cake. Top with second cake layer. Spread remaining filling over top of cake; top with third cake layer. Trim any uneven sides or edges to make perfect square-shaped box. Stir preserves and water in small saucepan over high heat until beginning to boil. Strain preserves into small bowl. Brush preserves over cake to coat completely. Refrigerate cake.

FOR THE FONDANT: Wearing gloves, knead food coloring, 1 drop at a time, into fondant until desired color is achieved. Wrap 1/4 of fondant in plastic; set aside. Sprinkle work surface and rolling pin with confectioners/powdered sugar. Flatten remaining fondant into square. Roll out fondant square into 26-inch square that is 1/4 inch thick, rotating to prevent sticking. Pierce bubbles that appear in fondant. Slide hands under fondant and drape over cake; smooth over surface. Trim excess fondant from around base of cake. Brush off excess confectioners/powdered sugar. Form reserved fondant into long rope. Roll out fondant rope into band 25 inches long by 2 1/2 inches wide. Trim band to 2-inch width. Using gum arabic as glue, wrap fondant band around top edge of cake to resemble box lid. Wrap ribbon around cake to resemble gift. Tie remaining ribbon into bow; place atop cake.

TROPICAL ISLAND BANANA CAKE

Serves 14

2	purchased (10 to 12 ounces each) angel food cakes
2	containers (16 ounces each) vanilla frosting, *Betty Crocker Rich & Creamy®*
1	teaspoon imitation banana extract, *McCormick®*
	Yellow food coloring
1	ripe banana, mashed
2	cups sweetened flaked coconut, *Baker's®*
1	cup fruit-shaped candies

Special Equipment:

1	palm tree decoration

Prep time: 15 minutes

P r e p a r a t i o n :

Place 1 cake, wide side down, on serving platter. Stir frosting and banana extract in large bowl to blend. Stir in yellow food coloring, 1 drop at a time, until desired color is achieved. Transfer 1/2 cup of banana frosting to small bowl; stir in mashed banana. Spread mashed banana mixture over top of cake. Cut one 2-inch-wide wedge from second cake. Spread 1/4 cup of banana frosting over cut ends of second cake. Bring cut ends of second cake together, pressing to adhere. Place second cake, wide side down, atop cake on platter. Tear cake wedge into cubes. Fill hole in center of cakes with cake cubes. Spread remaining banana frosting evenly over top and sides of cake to coat completely. Sprinkle cake with coconut, pressing lightly to adhere. Place palm tree decoration atop cake. Arrange fruit-shaped candy decoratively around palm tree and base of cake.

LIFE'S A BEACH CAKE

Serves 8

1	purchased (10-12-ounce) angel food cake
10	large marshmallows, *Kraft Jet-Puffed®*
2	containers (16 ounces each) vanilla frosting, *Betty Crocker Rich & Creamy®*
	Blue food coloring
1/2	cup sweetened flaked coconut, *Baker's®*

Special Equipment and Decorations:

Pastry bag; large star tip; 3 paper umbrellas; jellied octopus candy; chocolate seashell candy

Prep time: 15 minutes

P r e p a r a t i o n :

Place cake, wide side down, on serving platter. Fill hole in center of cake with marshmallows. Spread 1 1/2 containers of frosting evenly over top and sides of cake to coat completely. Stir food coloring, 1 drop at a time, into remaining 1/2 container of frosting until desired color is achieved. Transfer blue-colored frosting to pastry bag fitted with star tip. Pipe thick line of frosting around base of cake. Starting at base of cake and swirling in semicircular upward motion, drag wooden skewer through blue-colored frosting to form wave design. Arrange umbrellas on top. Arrange jellied candy octopus and chocolate seashells decoratively on cake. Sprinkle coconut around base of cake.

For the Holidays

RASPBERRY FONDUE WITH MERINGUE CLOUD HEARTS

Makes about 2 1/2 cups of fondue, and about 20 meringues

FONDUE

3/4	cup heavy cream
1	bag (12-ounce) premier white morsels, *Nestlé®*
2/3	cup seedless red raspberry jam
1/4	cup white chocolate liqueur, *Godiva®*
	Meringue Cloud Hearts (see recipe)

MERINGUE CLOUD HEARTS

2	egg whites, at room temperature
1/8	teaspoon cream of tartar, *McCormick®*
	Pinch of salt
1/2	cup granulated sugar
	Red and yellow food coloring

Special equipment:
Pastry bag
#2 star tip

Fondue prep time: 15 minutes
Meringue Cloud Hearts prep time: 15 minutes, baking time: 1 hour, cooling time: 20 minutes

Fondue Preparation:

Heat cream in medium saucepan over medium heat until bubbles appear; remove from heat. Add white morsels and whisk until melted and smooth. Stir in raspberry jam, then chocolate liqueur. Transfer mixture to fondue pot. To keep fondue warm at the table for an extended period, place over candle or canned heat burner. For eating immediately, serve in a decorative gravy boat. Serve fondue with Meringue Cloud Hearts for dipping.
Dipping Variations: Cubes of pound cake, fresh strawberries, marshmallows, or dried fruit.

Meringue Cloud Hearts Preparation:

Preheat oven to 200 degrees. Line 2 heavy large baking sheets with parchment paper. Place egg whites in clean large metal bowl. Beat on medium speed until foamy. Add cream of tartar and increase speed to high. Continue beating until soft peaks form. Mix in salt. gradually add sugar, 1 tablespoon at a time, beating until stiff peaks form, about 5 minutes. Quickly mix in food colorings, 1 drop at a time, until desired color is achieved. Transfer meringue to pastry bag fitted with star tip. Pipe 2-inch-diameter heart-shape meringues onto prepared baking sheets, spacing evenly apart. Bake for 1 hour, or until dry and crispy when broken in half. Cool meringues completely on baking sheets. Store in airtight container at room temperature.

STRAWBERRY CAKE WITH REAL STRAWBERRY FROSTING

This cake-on-a-cake confection is poetry on a plate. Topped with a seductive swirl of strawberry frosting and fresh berries, this red letter day dessert spells sweet romance any way you slice it.

Serves 8 to 10

CAKE:

1	box (18.25-ounce) strawberry cake mix, *Betty Crocker SuperMoist®*
1	can (11.5-ounce) strawberry nectar, *Kern's®*
3	eggs
1/4	cup vegetable oil

FILLING AND FROSTING:

2	containers (16 ounces each) strawberry frosting, *Betty Crocker Rich & Creamy®*
1	pound fresh strawberries, cleaned

Prep time:	10 minutes
Baking time:	25 minutes
Cooling time:	45 minutes
Chilling time:	40 minutes
Decorating time:	10 minutes

Cake Preparation:

Preheat oven to 350 degrees. Butter and flour two 9-inch-diameter round cake pans. Combine cake mix, nectar, eggs, and oil in large bowl. Beat for 2 minutes, or until well blended. Divide batter between prepared pans. Bake for 25 minutes, or until toothpick inserted into center of cakes comes out clean. Cool cakes in pans on cooling racks for 15 minutes. Invert cakes onto cooling rack and cool completely.

Filling and Frosting Preparation:

Slice enough strawberries to make 3/4 cup. Using serrated knife, cut each cake horizontally in half, forming 4 layers total. Place 1 cake layer, cut side down, on serving platter. Spread 1/3 cup of frosting over top of cake layer. Arrange 1/4 cup of sliced strawberries in single layer atop frosting. Top with second cake layer, cut side down. Repeat layering with frosting and sliced strawberries. Top with third cake layer, cut side down. Repeat layering with frosting and remaining sliced strawberries. Top with remaining cake layer, cut side down. Spread remaining frosting evenly over top and sides of cake to coat completely. Arrange sliced strawberries and 1 whole one decoratively atop cake. Refrigerate cake for 40 minutes. Serve cake with remaining whole strawberries.

EASTER BUNNY CAKE

Serves 8 to 10

CAKE AND FROSTING:

1	box (18.25-ounce) classic yellow cake mix, *Duncan Hines Moist Deluxe®*
1 1/3	cups water
1/3	cup vegetable oil
3	eggs
2	containers (16 ounces each) strawberry frosting, *Betty Crocker Rich & Creamy®*
1	bag (14-ounce) sweetened flaked coconut, *Baker's®*

DECORATIONS:

1/2	cup milk chocolate morsels, melted, *Nestlé®*
1	big chocolate chunk cookie, cut in half, *Pepperidge Farm®*
2	semi-sweet chocolate morsels, *Nestlé®*
1	sugar-coated gum drop candy
1	red licorice lace, cut into 6 equal pieces
2	miniature marshmallows, *Kraft Jet-Puffed®*
3	large marshmallows, *Kraft Jet-Puffed®*

Special equipment:
One 6-inch-diameter metal bowl, one 8-inch-diameter metal bowl, wooden toothpicks

Prep time: 30 minutes, baking time: 45 minutes, cooling time: 45 minutes
Decorating time: 20 minutes

Cake Preparation:

Preheat oven to 350 degrees. Butter and flour one 6-inch-diameter and one 8-inch-diameter metal bowl. Combine cake mix, water, oil, and eggs in another clean large bowl. Beat for 2 minutes or until well blended. Pour 2 cups of batter into smaller prepared bowl; pour remaining batter into larger prepared bowl. Bake smaller cake for 40 minutes and larger cake for 45 minutes, or until toothpick inserted into center of cakes comes out clean. Cool cakes in bowls on cooling rack for 30 minutes. Invert cakes onto cooling rack and cool completely.

DECORATING: Cut larger cake in half, forming 2 half-moon pieces. Spread 1/4 cup of frosting over flat top of each piece. Place pieces cut side down on work surface, adhering frosted sides together. Trim 1 inch from 1 end of cake; discard trimmings. Repeat with smaller cake. Place larger cake on serving platter. Spread 2 tablespoons of frosting over trimmed end of smaller cake. Place trimmed end of smaller cake against trimmed end of larger cake. Spread remaining frosting over cakes to cover completely. Sprinkle with all but 1/2 cup of coconut, pressing to adhere. Brush melted milk chocolate over both sides of cookie halves to coat completely. Sprinkle with reserved 1/2 cup of coconut; set aside until dry. Press two semi-sweet chocolate morsels onto bunny face for eyes. Using toothpick, secure jellied candy onto bunny face for nose. Using toothpicks, secure licorice pieces onto bunny face for whiskers. Using toothpicks, secure miniature marshmallows onto bunny face for teeth. Make 2-inch-deep cuts atop bunny head; insert chocolate cookie halves for ears. Roll large marshmallows together; using toothpick, secure onto bunny for tail.

EASTER BASKET ANGEL FOOD CAKE

This candy-covered cake can't miss with kids. Swap fresh flowers for the candy to turn the Easter Basket into a Spring Basket.

Serves 8

1	purchased (10- to 12-ounce) angel food cake
1	container (16-ounce) strawberry frosting, *Betty Crocker Rich & Creamy®*
3	red licorice twists
	Candy eggs

Special equipment:
One 18-inch-long piece of florist wire
Sugar flowers
Paper butterflies

Prep time: 15 minutes

P r e p a r a t i o n :

Place cake, narrow side down, on serving platter.

Spread all but 1 tablespoon of frosting evenly over tops and sides of cake to coat completely.

Trim 1/4 inch off ends of each licorice twist.

Thread florist wire through center of licorice twists.

Bend wire and licorice into "U" shape.

Insert wire ends into top of cake, to resemble basket handle.

Arrange candy eggs decoratively atop cake.

Arrange sugar flowers around base of cake.

Using reserved 1 tablespoon of frosting, adhere butterflies to licorice handle and cake.

Mother's Day

SPRING STRAWBERRY SHORTCAKE

Serves 6 to 8

4 2/3	cups all-purpose baking mix, *Bisquick®*
I	cup whole milk
1/4	cup plus I tablespoon butter, melted
1/4	cup plus I tablespoon granulated sugar
2	pounds fresh strawberries, sliced
I	container (16-ounce) frozen whipped topping, thawed, *Cool Whip®*
	Rose petals
	Additional whole fresh strawberries

Prep time:	10 minutes
Baking time:	10 minutes
Cooling time:	40 minutes
Assembly time:	10 minutes

Preparation:

Preheat oven to 425 degrees. Butter two 8-inch-diameter round baking pans. Combine baking mix, milk, 1/4 cup of butter, and 1/4 cup of sugar in large bowl. Mix just until soft dough forms. Press dough into prepared pans, dividing equally. Brush tops of dough with remaining I tablespoon of butter; sprinkle with remaining I tablespoon of sugar. Bake for 10 minutes, or until golden brown. Cool shortcakes in pans on cooling racks for 15 minutes. Invert shortcakes onto cooling racks and cool completely. Using potato masher, coarsely mash half of sliced strawberries in large bowl. Fold whipped topping into mashed berries; set berry cream aside.

TO ASSEMBLE: Using serrated knife, cut shortcakes horizontally in half. Reserve most attractive shortcake layer. Place I shortcake layer, cut side up, on serving platter. Top with 1/3 of berry cream, then with remaining 1/3 of sliced strawberries. Repeat layering 2 times. Top with reserved shortcake layer. Decorate with rose petals and whole strawberries. Serve immediately.

MOTHER'S DAY BONNET CAKE

Serves 14

2	purchased (10 to 12 ounces each) angel food cakes
2	containers (16 ounces each) vanilla frosting, *Betty Crocker Rich & Creamy®*
4	feet white wired ribbon (about 2 inches wide)
	Assorted edible fresh flowers (such as white rosebuds, lilies, and baby's breath), stems trimmed

Prep time:	15 minutes

Preparation:

Place I cake, wide side down, on serving platter. Spread thin layer of frosting over top of cake. Cut one 2-inch-wide wedge from second cake. Spread 1/4 cup of frosting over cut ends of second cake. Bring cut ends of second cake together, pressing to adhere. Place second cake atop cake on platter. Tear cake wedge into cubes. Fill hole in center of cakes with cake cubes. Spread remaining frosting evenly over top and sides of cake to coat completely. Tie ribbon around cake and form bow. Arrange flowers decoratively around base of cake to resemble hat rim.

FOURTH OF JULY ANGEL FOOD CAKE

Serves 14

2	purchased (10 to 12 ounces each) angel food cakes
2 1/2	containers (16 ounces each) vanilla frosting, *Betty Crocker Rich & Creamy®*
1	box (4.5-ounce) strawberry-flavored fruit snacks, *Betty Crocker Fruit by the Foot®*
1	pint fresh blueberries

Special Equipment and Decorations:
Pastry bag
Large star tip

Prep time: 15 minutes

Preparation:

Place 1 cake, wide side down, on serving platter. Spread thin layer of frosting over top of cake. Cut one 2-inch-wide wedge from second cake. Spread 1/4 cup of frosting over cut ends of second cake. Bring cut ends of second cake together, pressing to adhere. Place second cake atop cake on platter. Break cake wedge into cubes. Fill hole in center of cakes with cake cubes. Spread 1 whole container of frosting evenly over top and sides of cake to coat completely. Cut fruit roll strips to match height of cake. Press fruit roll strips vertically onto sides of cake to resemble stripes. Arrange blueberries decoratively atop cake. Transfer remaining frosting to pastry bag fitted with star tip. Pipe frosting decoratively around upper and lower edges of cake. Pipe stars atop blueberries.

APPLE CRISP PIE

Serves 6

1 1/2	cups cold whole milk
1	box (3.4-ounce) vanilla instant pudding and pie filling mix, *Jell-O®*
1 1/2	teaspoons ground cinnamon, *McCormick®*
1	(6-ounce) premade graham cracker pie crust, *Keebler Ready Crust®*
1	container (21-ounce) sliced apple pie filling or topping, *Comstock More Fruit®*
2	(1.5 ounces each) crunchy granola bars, *Nature Valley®*

Prep time: 10 minutes
Chilling time: 10 minutes

Preparation:

Combine milk, pudding mix, and 1 teaspoon of cinnamon in large bowl. Beat for 2 minutes, or until well blended and beginning to thicken. Pour into graham cracker pie crust. Refrigerate for 10 minutes. Stir apple pie filling with remaining 1/2 teaspoon of cinnamon in medium bowl to blend. Spread apple pie filling over pudding. Cover pie and refrigerate until ready to serve. Enclose granola bars in resealable plastic bag. Using rolling pin, crush bars into coarse crumbs. Sprinkle pie with granola crumbs and serve.

Halloween

CRUNCHY DONUT EYEBALLS

These terrifyingly tasty treats are loaded with squeal appeal. The trick is to use pre-packaged donut holes, dipped in white chocolate and decorated with M&M's® and Gummi Savers®. Scare up a plateful of these incredible edibles at your next Halloween party or send some to school with your little goblins. They're frightfully good fun for the office, too. What's really scary is they take only 30 minutes to make.

Makes 20

20	glazed donut holes, *Entenmann's®*
1	cup premier white morsels, *Nestlé®*
2	tablespoons solid vegetable shortening, *Crisco®*
20	*Life Savers Gummies®*
20	mini candy-coated milk chocolate candies, *M&M's Minis®*
2	drops red food coloring

Prep time:	30 minutes
Chilling time:	10 minutes

Preparation:

Line cookie sheet with parchment paper or wax paper. Cut 1/8-inch-thick slices from 2 opposite sides of each donut hole. Combine white morsels and vegetable shortening in medium metal bowl. Set bowl atop saucepan of simmering water and stir until morsels are melted and smooth. Using fork, and working with 1 donut hole at a time, dip donut holes into melted morsel mixture to coat. Lift coated donuts from melted morsel mixture, shaking excess coating back into bowl. Place coated donuts, 1 cut side down, on prepared cookie sheet. Place jellied candies atop coated donuts. Dab chocolate candies with some of remaining melted morsel mixture and press onto jellied candies to form eyeballs. Refrigerate for 10 minutes, or until coating is set. Stir 2 drops of food coloring and 2 tablespoons of melted morsel mixture in small bowl to blend. Using toothpick, paint colored morsel mixture on donut eyeballs to resemble veins. Refrigerate until ready to serve.

for the holidays
Halloween

HALLOWEEN PUMPKIN CAKE

Serves 14

2   purchased (10 to 12 ounces each) angel food cakes
       Red and yellow food coloring
2   containers (16 ounces each) vanilla frosting, *Betty Crocker Rich & Creamy*®
16   chocolate sandwich cookies, *Oreo*®
14   large marshmallows, *Kraft Jet-Puffed*®
1   container (8-ounce) frozen whipped topping, thawed, *Cool Whip*®
1   small *Tootsie Roll*®, cut in half

Special Equipment and Decorations:
Pastry bag, large plain tip

Prep time: 15 minutes

Preparation:

Place 1 cake, narrow side down, on serving platter. Stir food colorings, 1 drop at a time, into frosting in large bowl until desired orange color is achieved. Spread thin layer of frosting over top of cake. Place second cake, narrow side up, atop first cake to form pumpkin shape. Spread remaining frosting evenly over top and sides of cakes to coat completely. Break cookies apart; scrape off filling. Enclose cookies in resealable plastic bag. Using rolling pin, crush cookies into fine crumbs. Sprinkle chocolate cookie crumbs atop cake and around base of cake. Skewer marshmallows atop each other on wooden skewer. Place marshmallow skewer in hole in center of cake. Spoon whipped topping into pastry bag fitted with plain tip. Pipe whipped topping over marshmallow stack to resemble ghost. Shape one *Tootsie Roll*® piece into two small scary shapes for eyes. Shape second Tootsie Roll piece into scary shape for mouth. Place eyes and mouth on ghost.

CARAMEL PARFAITS

Makes 8

1   cup boiling water
1   box (3-ounce) instant orange gelatin dessert mix, *Jell-O*®
1   cup cold water
4   containers (3.5 ounces each) prepared butterscotch-flavored pudding, *Kraft Handi-Snacks*®
1   cup frozen whipped topping, thawed, *Cool Whip*®

Special Decorations:
Assorted halloween candies

Prep time: 15 minutes
Chilling time: 2 hours

Preparation:

Combine 1 cup of boiling water and gelatin mix in large bowl; stir until gelatin dissolves. Stir 1 cup of cold water into gelatin. Divide gelatin equally among 8 parfait or champagne glasses. Refrigerate for 2 hours, or until gelatin is set. Spoon butterscotch pudding atop gelatin in glasses, dividing equally. Spoon 2 tablespoons of whipped topping over pudding in each glass.

for the holidays

Halloween

MINI PUMPKIN SPICE CAKES WITH ORANGE GLAZE

Makes 8

CAKE:

1	box (18.25-ounce) spice cake mix, *Betty Crocker SuperMoist®*
1 1/4	cups water
1/3	cup vegetable oil
3	eggs

ORANGE GLAZE:

2/3	cup heavy cream
1	bag (12-ounce) premier white morsels, *Nestlé*
	Red and yellow food coloring

MARZIPAN STEMS AND LEAVES:

1	package (7-ounce) marzipan, *Odense®*
	Green food coloring

Special Equipment:
Disposable latex gloves, leaf-shaped cookie cutter

Prep time: 20 minutes, baking time: 20 minutes, cooling time: 30 minutes
Chilling time: 10 minutes, decorating time: 15 minutes

Cake Preparation:

Preheat oven to 350 degrees. Oil and flour 8 mini bundt pans. Combine cake mix, water, oil, and eggs in large bowl. Beat for 2 minutes, or until well blended. Divide batter equally among prepared pans. Bake for 20 minutes, or until toothpick inserted near center of cakes comes out clean. Cool cakes in pans on cooling racks for 15 minutes. Invert cakes onto cooling rack and cool completely. Set cooling rack atop baking sheet.

FOR THE ORANGE GLAZE: Heat cream in small saucepan over medium heat until bubbles appear; remove from heat. Add white morsels and stir until melted and smooth. Stir in food colorings, 1 drop at a time, until desired color is achieved. Drizzle glaze over cakes. Refrigerate cakes for 10 minutes, or until glaze is firm. Cover and reserve any remaining glaze.

FOR THE MARZIPAN STEMS AND LEAVES:

Place marzipan in medium bowl. Using latex gloves, knead food coloring, 1 drop at a time, into marzipan until desired color is achieved. Divide marzipan into 2 equal pieces. Roll 1 marzipan piece into 12-inch-long log. Cut log crosswise into 8 equal pieces; set aside to use as stems. Flatten remaining marzipan piece, then place between 2 sheets of plastic wrap. Using rolling pin, roll out marzipan to 1/4-inch thickness. Using leaf-shaped cookie cutter or small sharp knife, cut out 24 leaves. Decorate cakes with marzipan stems and leaves. Rewarm reserved glaze. Serve cakes, passing glaze alongside.

AUTUMN HARVEST CAKE

Serves 8

CAKE AND FROSTING:
1	purchased (10- to 12-ounce) angel food cake
1	container (16-ounce) vanilla frosting, *Betty Crocker Rich & Creamy®*
2	tablespoons unsweetened cocoa powder, *Hershey's®*
2	teaspoons pure vanilla extract, *McCormick®*
1	teaspoon ground cinnamon, *McCormick®*
1	container (21-ounce) apple pie filling or topping, *Comstock More Fruit®*
1	package (1.7-ounce) *Cornnuts®*
1/2	cup toasted pumpkin seeds

CHOCOLATE LEAVES:
1/2	cup semi-sweet chocolate morsels, *Nestlé®*
1/2	cup milk chocolate morsels, *Nestlé®*

Special equipment:
Twenty lemon leaves, washed and dried well

Prep time:	15 minutes
Chilling time:	20 minutes

Preparation:

Using serrated knife, cut cake horizontally into 2 layers. Place bottom cake layer, cut side up, on serving platter. Mix frosting, cocoa powder, vanilla, and cinnamon in large bowl to blend. Spread some frosting over top of cake. Top with remaining cake layer, cut side down. Spread remaining frosting evenly over top and sides of cake to coat completely. Fill center hole with apple pie filling. Sprinkle top of cake with some *Cornnuts®* and pumpkin seeds. Scatter remaining *Cornnuts®* and pumpkin seeds around base of cake.

FOR THE CHOCOLATE LEAVES:

Line cookie sheet with parchment or waxed paper. Melt each kind of chocolate separately in microwave for 1 1/2 minutes, stirring every 30 seconds, or until smooth. Using offset spatula, spread underside of leaves with melted chocolates. Place leaves, chocolate side up, on prepared cookie sheet. Do not allow chocolate to drip over leaf edges. Refrigerate until set, then peel away leaf. Arrange chocolate leaves decoratively atop cake.

SWEET POTATO PIE WITH MARSHMALLOW CREME

Serves 6

1	(6-ounce) premade graham cracker pie crust, *Keebler Ready Crust*®
1	can (15-ounce) candied sweet potatoes in syrup, drained, *Princess*®, or pure pumpkin, *Libby's*®
1	can (14-ounce) sweetened condensed milk, *Carnation*®
3	eggs
2	teaspoons pumpkin pie spice, *McCormick*®
1	jar (7-ounce) marshmallow creme, *Kraft Jet-Puffed*®
12	whole pecans, toasted

Special Equipment:
Kitchen torch (optional)

Prep time: 10 minutes, baking time: 35 minutes, cooling time: 1 hour

Preparation:

Preheat oven to 350 degrees. Place crust on heavy baking sheet. Blend sweet potatoes or pumpkin, condensed milk, eggs, and pie spice in blender until smooth. Pour mixture into crust. Bake for 35 minutes, or until filling puffs around edges and center is just set. Transfer pie to cooling rack and cool to room temperature. Just before serving, spread marshmallow creme over pie. If desired, use kitchen torch to quickly caramelize marshmallow cream. Garnish with pecans. Serve pie immediately.

MAPLE SYRUP PECAN PIE

Serves 8

1 1/4	cups maple flavored pancake syrup, *Log Cabin Original Syrup*®
1/3	cup (packed) golden brown sugar
3	eggs
1	egg yolk
2	teaspoons all purpose flour
1 1/2	teaspoons pure vanilla extract, *McCormick*®
2	tablespoons butter, melted
1	9-inch frozen unbaked deep-dish pie shell, *Marie Calendar's*®
1 1/2	cups pecan halves

Prep time: 10 minutes, baking time: 50 minutes, cooling time: 15 minutes

Preparation:

Preheat oven to 350 degrees. Stir maple syrup, sugar, eggs, egg yolk, flour, and vanilla in large bowl to blend. Whisk in melted butter (maple mixture will be very thin at this point). Stir in 1 cup of pecans. Place frozen pie shell on heavy baking sheet. Carefully pour maple mixture into pie shell. Arrange remaining 1/2 cup of pecans atop maple mixture, pressing into maple mixture to coat. Place baking sheet in center of oven. Bake pie for 50 minutes, or until crust edges are golden and filling is just set in center. Cool pie on cooling rack for 15 minutes. Cut pie into wedges and serve warm or at room temperature.

STAR OF DAVID ANGEL FOOD CAKE

An inexpensive faux pearl choker and Star of David topper make this easy angel food cake the star attraction at your holiday table. Just remove the pearls before cutting the cake, so nobody swallows one!

Serves 8

1	purchased (10- to 12-ounce) angel food cake
10	large marshmallows, *Kraft Jet-Puffed®*
	Blue food coloring
1	container (12-ounce) fluffy white frosting, *Betty Crocker Whipped®*

Special Equipment:
Wired pearl strands

Prep time: 15 minutes

P r e p a r a t i o n :

Place cake, wide side down, on serving platter.

Fill hole in center of cake with marshmallows.

Stir food coloring, 1 drop at a time, into frosting in large bowl until desired color is achieved.

Spread frosting evenly over top and sides of cake to coat completely.

Bend pearl strand into 2 Stars of David, leaving 2 inches of wire hanging down from bottom of each star.

Place 1 Star of David inside and perpendicular to second Star of David, creating 3-D effect.

Stand Stars of David atop cake.

Drape another pearl strand around base of cake.

Remove pearls before cutting and serving.

Variation: Place the Stars of David atop the cake along with 9 silver candles.

for the holidays
Hanukkah

BUTTERY HONEY CAKE

Serves 12 to 16

1	box (18.25-ounce) classic yellow cake mix, *Duncan Hines Moist Deluxe®*
1	cup water
1/3	cup plus 1/4 cup honey, *Sue Bee®*
1/3	cup margarine, melted
1/3	cup poppy seeds, *McCormick®*
3	eggs
1/2	teaspoon pumpkin pie spice, *McCormick®*
1/3	cup confectioners/powdered sugar, sifted

Prep time: 10 minutes, baking time: 45 minutes, cooling time: 30 minutes

Preparation:

Preheat oven to 350 degrees. Oil and flour 10-inch-diameter round cake pan with 2-inch-high sides. Combine cake mix, water, 1/3 cup of honey, margarine, poppy seeds, eggs, and pie spice in large bowl. Beat for 2 minutes, or until well blended. Pour into prepared pan. Bake for 45 minutes, or until toothpick inserted into center of cake comes out clean. Cool cake in pan on cooling rack for 15 minutes. Invert cake onto cooling rack and cool completely. Using wooden or metal skewer, poke about 20 small holes all over top of cake. Drizzle remaining 1/4 cup of honey over cake, allowing honey to sink into holes. Just before serving, dust with confectioners/powdered sugar.

KUGEL CRUMBLE

Kugel is traditionally served on the Jewish Sabbath, as either a savory side dish or dessert, but this comfy concoction is heavenly on any holiday. The crunchy "crumble" comes from crushed macaroons, baked to a golden brown.

Serves 8 to 10

	Nonstick cooking spray, *PAM®*
4	cups dried egg noodles, *American Beauty®*
12	macaroon cookies, *Mother's®*
1/2	cup dried apricots, *Sunsweet®*
2 1/2	cups whole milk
1	can (14-ounce) sweetened condensed milk, *Carnation®*
2	eggs
1/8	teaspoon grated nutmeg, *McCormick®*
1/4	cup honey, *Sue Bee®*

Prep time: 10 minutes, baking time: 35 minutes

Preparation:

Preheat oven to 350 degrees. Spray 8-inch-square baking dish with cooking spray. Cook noodles in large pot of boiling water until tender but still firm to bite. Drain in colander. Enclose macaroons in resealable plastic bag. Using rolling pin, crush macaroons into coarse crumbs. Using scissors sprayed with cooking spray, cut apricots into small pieces. Stir whole milk, condensed milk, eggs, and nutmeg in large bowl until well blended. Stir noodles and apricots into custard to coat completely. Transfer noodle mixture to prepared baking dish. Sprinkle macaroon crumbs over noodle mixture. Spray crumbs with cooking spray. Bake for 35 minutes, or until top is golden brown. Drizzle with honey and serve warm.

NUTCRACKER HOLIDAY CAKE

This whimsical cake looks like it was baked by the Sugar Plum Fairy, but you can whip it up at home in less time than it takes to drive to the bakery. It tastes like a giant gingerbread cookie, frosted with swirling snowflakes of cream cheese and topped with wooden nutcrackers and tiny wrapped gifts sure to capture the fancy of young and old. (Both the nutcracker and gift decorations are available at craft stores like Michaels.) This charming confection makes a delightful centerpiece dessert throughout the holidays, but it's especially magical on Christmas Eve, when you can tell the Nutcracker story and send everyone to bed with sweet dreams.

Serves 10 to 12

2	boxes (14.5 ounces each) gingerbread cake and cookie mix, *Krusteaz®*
2	cups water
2	eggs
1 1/2	containers (16 ounces each) cream cheese frosting, *Betty Crocker Rich & Creamy®*

Special Equipment:
Wrapped present decorations
Small wooden nutcrackers

Prep time:	10 minutes
Baking time:	30 minutes
Cooling time:	30 minutes

Preparation:

Preheat oven to 350 degrees.
Butter and flour two 8-inch-diameter round cake pans.
Combine cake mixes, water, and eggs in large bowl.
Beat for 2 minutes, or until well blended.
Divide batter between prepared pans.
Bake for 30 minutes, or until toothpick inserted into center of cakes comes out clean.
Cool cakes in pans on cooling rack for 15 minutes.
Invert cakes onto cooling racks and cool completely.
Place 1 cake layer on platter; spread 1/2 cup of frosting over top of cake.
Top with second cake layer, flat side up.
Spread remaining frosting over top and sides of cake to coat completely.
Decorate cake with wrapped presents and wooden nutcrackers.

SPICY WREATH FRUITCAKE

Serves 12 to 16

12	ounces mixed glacé fruit, chopped
1/2	cup chopped walnuts, toasted
1/3	cup chopped pitted dates, *Sunsweet®*
1	box (18.25-ounce) spice cake mix, *Betty Crocker SuperMoist®*
1 1/4	cups water
1/3	cup vegetable oil
3	eggs
2	teaspoons pure orange extract, *McCormick®*
2	teaspoons brandy extract, *McCormick®*
	Frozen whipped topping, thawed, *Cool Whip®* (optional)

Special Equipment:
Holiday ribbon (optional)

Prep time: 10 minutes, baking time: 45 minutes, cooling time: 30 minutes

Preparation:

Preheat oven to 350 degrees. Butter and flour 10-inch-diameter ring mold. Combine glacé fruit, walnuts, dates, and 3 tablespoons of dry cake mix in medium bowl; toss to coat. Combine remaining cake mix, water, oil, and eggs in large bowl. Beat for 2 minutes, or until well blended. Stir in orange and brandy extracts. Stir fruit and nut mixture into batter. Transfer batter to prepared mold. Bake for 45 minutes, or until toothpick inserted near center of cake comes out clean. Cool cake in pan on cooling rack for 15 minutes. Invert cake onto cooling rack and cool completely. Serve with a dollop of *Cool Whip®* (optional).

Tip: This cake can be made one week ahead. Wrap airtight with plastic and freeze.

CLASSIC HOLIDAY WREATH CAKE

Serves 8

1	purchased (10- to 12-ounce) angel food cake
	Green food coloring
1	container (16-ounce) vanilla frosting, *Betty Crocker Rich & Creamy®*
2	cups sweetened flaked coconut, *Baker's®*
3	purchased sugar leaf decorations, *Dec-A-Cake®*, or green decorating gel, *Cake Mate®*
3	hard cinnamon-flavored candies, *Red Hots®*, or red decorating gel, *Cake Mate®*

Special Equipment:
Disposable latex gloves, leaf-shaped cookie cutter (optional)

Prep time: 15 minutes

Preparation:

Place cake, wide side down, on serving platter. Stir food coloring, 1 drop at a time, into frosting in large bowl until desired color is achieved. Spread frosting evenly over top and sides of cake to coat completely. Press coconut into frosting to resemble snow. Arrange candy leaves atop cake, or pipe green gel atop cake to resemble holly leaves. Arrange cinnamon candies atop cake, or pipe red gel atop cake to resemble holly berries.

Variation: Marizpan can be used to make your own holly leaves. Place marzipan in medium metal bowl. Using disposable gloves, knead food coloring, 1 drop at a time, into marzipan until desired color is achieved. Flatten marzipan piece, then place between 2 sheets of plastic wrap. Using rolling pin, roll out marzipan to 1/2-inch thickness. Using small sharp knife or holly leaf-shaped cookie cutter, cut out leaves.

WHITE CHOCOLATE YULE LOG WITH SNOW FROSTING

Makes 2 yule logs, 8 to 10 slices each

CAKE:
1	box (18.25-ounce) Swiss chocolate cake mix, *Duncan Hines Moist Deluxe®*
1 1/4	cups water
1/2	cup vegetable oil
3	eggs
1/4	cup confectioners/powdered sugar

FILLING AND FROSTING:
1	container (16-ounce) frozen whipped topping, thawed, *Cool Whip®*
1	container (12-ounce) fluffy white frosting, *Betty Crocker Whipped®*

FOREST MUSHROOMS:
10	chocolate Kisses, unwrapped, *Hershey's®*
10	miniature marshmallows, *Kraft Jet-Puffed®*
1/4	cup confectioners/powdered sugar

Prep time: 15 minutes, baking time: 15 minutes, cooling time: 20 minutes
Freezing time: 30 minutes, decorating time: 10 minutes

Cake Preparation:

Position 1 rack in upper third of oven and second rack in center of oven; preheat to 350 degrees. Line two 13 x 9 x 3/4-inch baking sheets with parchment paper, allowing 1 inch of paper to hang over sides. Combine cake mix, water, oil, and eggs in large bowl. Beat for 2 minutes, or until well blended. Divide batter between prepared pans; spread to cover pan evenly. Bake for 15 minutes, or until toothpick inserted into center of cakes comes out clean, rotating pans halfway through baking. Sift confectioners/powdered sugar over hot cakes. Working with 1 hot cake at a time, place clean kitchen towel atop cake. Place cutting board (which is larger than baking sheet) atop towel on cake. Invert cake onto towel and cutting board. Remove pan and carefully peel off parchment paper. Starting at 1 long side and using towel as aid, gently roll up cake jelly-roll style (cake will crack). Repeat with second cake. Cool rolled cakes completely.

FOR THE FILLING AND FROSTING: Unroll cakes. Spread whipped topping evenly over cakes. Roll up cakes (not towel) jelly-roll style, enclosing filling. Arrange cakes seam side down on serving platters. Freeze cakes for 30 minutes, or until firm (this will make them easier to frost). Spread white frosting over cakes to coat completely. Draw fork along length of cakes to form bark design. Refrigerate cakes.

FOR THE FOREST MUSHROOMS: Using small sharp knife, round tips of Kisses slightly to resemble mushroom cap. Insert 1 toothpick through each marshmallow, then into flat side of chocolate mushroom cap. Place chocolate mushrooms on cakes. Dust with confectioners/powdered sugar.

HARVEST WALNUT COOKIES

Makes about 6 dozen

VANILLA DOUGH:

I	box (18.25-ounce) white cake mix, *Betty Crocker SuperMoist®*
1/3	cup vegetable oil
4	tablespoons butter, melted
I	egg, beaten to blend
I	teaspoon pure vanilla extract, *McCormick®*
3/4	cup chopped walnuts, lightly toasted

CHOCOLATE DOUGH:

I	box (18.25-ounce) devil's food cake mix, *Betty Crocker SuperMoist®*
1/3	cup vegetable oil
4	tablespoons butter, melted
I	egg, beaten to blend
2	teaspoons pure vanilla extract, *McCormick®*
3/4	cup chopped walnuts, lightly toasted

Prep time:	20 minutes
Baking time:	30 minutes

Vanilla Dough Preparation:

Beat cake mix, oil, melted butter, egg, and vanilla in large bowl until dough forms.
Stir in walnuts.

Chocolate Dough Preparation:

Beat cake mix, oil, melted butter, egg, and vanilla in large bowl until dough forms.
Stir in walnuts.

Cookie Preparation:

Preheat oven to 400 degrees.
Scoop I teaspoon of vanilla dough into ball.
Scoop I teaspoon of chocolate dough into ball.
Gently press dough balls together, then roll gently to form one ball.
Place 20 balls on heavy large ungreased baking sheet, spacing evenly apart.
Bake for 10 minutes, or just until cookies begin to brown.
Cool cookies on cookie sheets for 5 minutes.
Transfer cookies to cooling racks and cool completely.
Repeat with remaining chocolate and vanilla doughs, forming about 6 dozen cookies total.
Store in airtight container at room temperature up to 2 days, or freeze up to 3 months.

for the holidays

Kwanzaa

SWEET BLESSINGS APPLE CAKE

Serves 8 to 10

1	box (15-ounce) honey cornbread & muffin mix, *Krusteaz*®
1	cup whole milk
2	eggs
2	tablespoons yellow cornmeal, *Albers*®
1	container (21-ounce) apple pie filling or topping, *Comstock More Fruit*®
1 1/2	cups low fat granola, *Kellogg's*®
3/4	cup honey, warmed, *Sue Bee*®

Prep time: 20 minutes, baking time: 40 minutes, cooling time: 10 minutes

Preparation:

Preheat oven to 400 degrees. Butter 9-inch-square baking pan. Combine cornbread mix, milk, eggs, and cornmeal in large bowl. Stir until just moistened; stir in apple filling. Transfer batter to prepared pan. Sprinkle granola over batter. Set aside for 15 minutes. Bake for 40 minutes, or until toothpick inserted into center of cake comes out clean. Cool cake for 10 minutes. Drizzle warm honey over warm cake and serve.

KWANZAA CELEBRATION CAKE

Serves 8

1	purchased (10- to 12-ounce) angel food cake
1	container (16-ounce) vanilla frosting, *Betty Crocker Rich & Creamy*®
2	tablespoons unsweetened cocoa powder, *Hershey's*®
2	teaspoons pure vanilla extract, *McCormick*®
1	teaspoon ground cinnamon, *McCormick*®
1	container (21-ounce) apple pie filling or topping, *Comstock More Fruit*®
1	package (1.7-ounce) *Cornnuts*®
1/2	cup toasted pumpkin seeds
1/2	cup popped popcorn

Special Equipment:
Kwanzaa candles

Prep time: 15 minutes

Preparation:

Using serrated knife, cut cake horizontally into 2 layers. Place bottom cake layer, cut side up, on serving platter. Mix frosting, cocoa powder, vanilla, and cinnamon in large bowl to blend. Spread some frosting over top of cake layer on platter. Top with second cake layer, cut side down. Spread remaining frosting evenly over top and sides of cake to coat completely. Spoon apple pie filling into hole in center of cake. Place candles atop cake. Sprinkle top of cake with some *Cornnuts*®, pumpkin seeds, and popcorn. Sprinkle remaining *Cornnuts*®and pumpkin seeds around base of cake.

For the Host

HELPFUL HINTS, TIPS, AND TRICKS

Entertaining is easy—all it takes is a little know-how and ingenuity. Creative gatherings are what this chapter is all about. The secret is to keep the basics simple and let details make the difference. The following items can be reused again and again, and many can even decorate your home when they're not in use. Greenery, serving plates, and cake pedestals add interest to cabinet tops, and gold frames look perfect propped against walls and mantels. The rest can be tucked into a "party cabinet," where they're easy to reach when it's time to entertain.

Must haves: Simple white dinnerware; matching white serving plates; glass stemware—water glasses, wine goblets, and champagne flutes; flatware; serving spoons and forks; 18 clear glass votive holders with white candles; stackable cake stand pedestals (in 8", 10", and 12" sizes).

Decorative extras: Fabric remnants for tablecloths; ribbons; spray paint (in a selection of colors); ornate gold frames (16" x 20" oval, 24" x 30" rectangular); fabric ivy or greenery; 3" terra-cotta pots.

Over time: Gold and silver chargers; votive candles in a variety of colors (watch for sales and stock up); glass stemware—martini, margarita, and shot glasses; individual clear glass cake pedestals.

Note: A tiny bit of creativity and imagination will go a long way toward creating a cost-conscious, picture-perfect *Semi-Homemade*® party.

Special thanks to: Petals and Wax, Pier One, Rosebud Cakes, and Hotel Bel-Air.

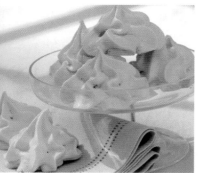

Gorgeous Garden Party

Theme: A mixed bouquet of colors makes a gorgeous picked-from-the-garden setting for a Mother's Day luncheon, warm-weather brunch or stylish tea party.

Dessert Centerpiece: Serve dessert in high style by stacking three tiers of glass cake pedestals, each filled with deliciously drippy cupcakes iced with the word "tea" in pretty pastels (for tea cake recipe, see p. 19). The cake topper is a sundae glass filled with multicolored hydrangeas, ringed with mint meringues (for meringue recipe, see p. 122).

Decorative Detail: A pale blue tablecloth makes a serene backdrop to mint green napkins and petite cake pedestals bearing mint meringues. A curl of green ribbon across each plate is the finishing touch.

Place Card: A personal handwritten note slipped into a matching envelope and propped against each guest's beverage glass makes company feel special.

Beverage: Ice-blended limeade is garnished with sprigs of fresh mint and served in iridescent blue glasses that catch the light. Colored straws complete the watercolor effect.

Music: Mozart, "Great Piano Concertos"; London Symphony Orchestra, "Victoria's Secret Classics"

Floral Favor: My girlfriend Barbara makes favors as charming as she is. Large yellow and blue flowered tea cups overflow with brightly hued hydrangeas, adding a grace note to the table and sending guests home with cheery memories of a delightful day. A bring-home box of bon bons is another sweet treat for partygoers. To make, simply glue silk purple posies on top of small white boxes from the stationery store and fill with store-bought chocolates.

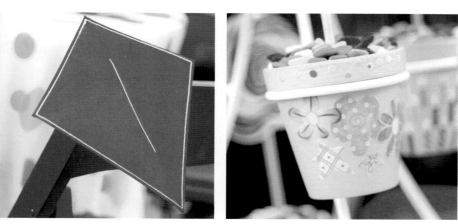

Theme: Bright bubblegum colors and a treasure trove of sweet eats make a child's birthday party an imaginative retreat.

Favor Centerpiece: Whimsical take-home lollipop pots will draw admiring eyes—and eager hands—when filled with colorful candy and gumballs. So easy to make: Buy an herb garden planter from *Pier 1®*, spray paint the stand white and the pots in a rainbow of colors. To set each pot "abloom," decorate with fun stickers, glue floral foam in the bottom, insert a large swirl lollipop and shovel in candy.

Decorative Detail: The polka-dot tablecloth is a king-size flat sheet. Red folding chairs cost little to rent; add detail with miniature kites taped to the back. Colorful inexpensive curly ribbons are cut from the roll and hung in the trees.

Dessert and Drink: Cotton Candy Bombs make a creative alternative to cake, and ingredients are store-bought to keep party prep simple. Arrange small scoops of strawberry and bubblegum ice cream on each plate, place a cloud of cotton candy on top, add a scoop of ice cream in the center and insert a candle. The party punch is an old favorite—*Hawaiian Punch®* mixed with *7 UP®*.

Place Setting: Plastic tableware and paper napkins in mix-and-match colors make cleanup a breeze. Candy bracelet napkin rings and multicolored plastic souvenir *Slinky®* toys make fun favors.

Music: *Richard M. Sherman, "Mary Poppins: An Original Walt Disney Records Soundtrack"; The Archies, "Sugar, Sugar"*

Theme: An exotic tapestry of earth tones and textures make this Arabian Nights buffet a romantic choice for a sunset soiree, engagement party, or couples night out.

Decorative Detail: Silky sari curtain panels cover the table. Sari wraps sway seductively from the trees, creating a tentlike intimacy, and are used to cover pillows, which are scattered on the floor for casual seating, Middle Eastern style. Faux jeweled bracelets serve as napkin rings. Presiding over the buffet is an inexpensive fiberglass statue of Quan Yin, the Chinese goddess of mercy and compassion, flanked by small iron *Pier 1®* candle screens, whose tiny white candles beckon guests to the table.

Food and Drink: Food is easy with Moroccan take-out—couscous, lamb skewers, roast chicken, and fruit—making a vivid counterpart to brick-colored pedestal bowls, and platters. Red wine is served in pale pink glasses with gold etching—an exotic departure from traditional wine glasses. Phyllo Pie Bites are a sensually sweet nightcap of chocolate and cherry (for recipe, see p. 28).

Music: *London Symphony Orchestra, "Rimsky-Korsakov: Scheherazade/Capriccio Espagnol"; David Visan, "Buddha Bar"*

Firelight: A flickering flame ups the romance. The fire pit is a metal bucket with a ceramic planter full of kindling slipped inside. A long wrought iron votive holder holds soft pink candles.

Theme: Shades of orange and black and gore galore create a frightfully festive setting for your Halloween haunting.

Beastly Buffet Centerpiece: Here's an easy way to protect guests from snack attacks. Take an herb garden planter from *Pier 1®*, spray paint it black, roll orange paper into cones and insert one per pot; fill with caramel popcorn, crunchy eyeballs and store-bought candy corn. Glue a foam black bat on top, drape with spider webbing and surround with black votives.

Devilish Dessert and Drink Buffet: Even Dracula couldn't resist a bite of these devilicious delights. An orange-frosted ghost cake, caramel parfaits, and mini *Oreos®* served in Halloween baking cups make cool ghoul gruel. Downscale caramel apples to bite-size portions by dipping petite Lady or crab apples in caramel and rolling in nuts, candy, and crushed cookies. Conjure up a plastic pumpkin filled with Witches Brew—equal parts 7 *UP®* and lemonade, tinted a ghastly green with food coloring. Add spooky smoke by placing dry ice at the bottom of the pumpkins and setting the punch bowl inside (use medium size *Pyrex®* bowl). Use mini plastic pumpkins for cups. (For recipes, see pp. 158-162.)

Macabre Music: *Franz Liszt, "Fright Night: Music That Goes Bump in the Night"; Various Artists, "Halloween Hits"*

Diabolical Detail: Lure guests into your chamber of horrors with hand-lettered invitations decorated with a glued-on spider. To get your crypt crawling with charm, drape torn fishnet stockings and icky sticky spider webbing from windows and walls; add a ghostly glow with Chinese paper lanterns spray painted orange and black. Drape the buffet in orange fabric, accenting with black paper napkins and orange terra-cotta pots filled with black plastic utensils.

Sandra's niece Danielle makes a positively perfect pecan pie.

Theme: Autumn colors and fruits of the harvest welcome family and friends for a grateful gathering.

Centerpiece: A black coffee press is filled with fragrant coffee beans and tall cattails, a homey reminder of nature's bounty.

Decorative Detail: The table becomes the epitome of plenty when scattered with oranges, kumquats, mini squash, pumpkins, and pinecones. A gold frame hangs behind the buffet, which is draped with a faux silk remnant. A wooden barrel holds wine bottles; a coffee press overflows with fiery-hued autumn leaves. On the main table, turkey-shaped gravy bowls hold store-bought chocolate-covered coffee beans.

Dessert Buffet: Mini pumpkin spice cakes (recipe p. 162), sweet potato pies (recipe p. 166), and pecan caramel cheesecake (recipe p. 23) are a mixture of sugar and spice. Beautiful bonbons are simply small scoops of ice cream dunked in melted chocolate chips. (For melting instructions, see *Helpful Hints, Tips, and Tricks*, p. 35).

Place Setting: The table is definitely down-home—pinking-sheared brown corduroy fabric for a tablecloth, squash-yellow tableware, and napkins tied with leather shoelaces. The place cards are tiny *Hallmark®* booklets titled for each family member (mom, dad, etc.).

Music: *Various Artists, "Thanksgiving: A Wyndham Hill Collection"; Vivaldi et al., "A Classic Thanksgiving: We Gather Together"*

Drink: To make heartwarming wassail for four, blend two cups of light rum, 1/2 cup dark rum, five 25-oz. bottles of sparkling apple cider, and one 64-oz. carton of mango juice. Clothespin a silk leaf to the goblet stem.

195

Austen and his Aunt Sandra snuggle together, enjoying their family's holiday season gathering.

Theme: Burgundy and gold give a rich twist to a traditional Christmas.
Decorative Detail: Burgundy feather trees sprayed with gold glitter adhesive sparkle behind a "chandelier" of faux crystal garlands draped from the ceiling. Burgundy hurricanes and gold votives cast a starry light over a simple gold tablecloth, overlaid with sequined gold sheering.
Dessert and Drink: A dazzling feast of fruitcake and cheesecake is both naughty and nice. (For recipes, see pp. 175 & 23.) To create visions of sugar plums, scoop cheesecake into balls, insert a lollipop stick and dip in white chocolate, nuts, and caramels. A merry little merlot, infused with store-bought mulling spices, is garnished with a tiny ornament on a gold straw.
Place Setting: Clear glass plates are dressed up with inexpensive gold chargers and burgundy napkins wrapped in faux crystal garlands. Burgundy ribbon curls around the plates and petite cake pedestals holding store-bought ornament ball cakes.
Floral Favor: To give guests sweet dreams, spray paint stationery store boxes gold, glue a burgundy fabric rose on top and mist with gold glitter adhesive; fill with gilded chocolate almonds.
Music: *Tchaikovsky, "The Nutcracker - Complete Ballet"; Charlotte Church et al., "Our Favorite Things"*

Centerpiece: Four stacked squares of moss-covered *Styrofoam®* rest on pedestals of burgundy glass ornament balls. Burgundy organza wire ribbon cascades from the top, which is decorated with painted *Styrofoam®* berries, ice skater ornaments, and festive dragonflies.

Theme: Whether it's a brand new year or a black tie ball, shimmery silver and white let you celebrate in style.

Centerpiece: The best-dressed tables are wearing a head-turning centerpiece of fashionable white feathers. It's easy to make: Sprinkle a tall, clear vase with iridescent glitter, fill it 2/3 with rock salt and insert 10-12 white plume feathers.

Decorative Detail: Special occasions call for glitz and glamour, so go all out. Make a festive backdrop by tacking silver lamé to the walls and attaching strands of silver disco ball beading (available at most party stores). Give plain white plates pizzazz with silver chargers and a veil of silver mesh netting draped over each place setting. Sprinkle the table with iridescent glitter, add iridescent white tea candles in clear votives, and scatter silver ball ornaments and silvered almonds around the table. (On New Year's Eve, tune in to Dick Clark's "Rockin' New Year's Eve" countdown.)

Dessert and Drink: The toast of the party will be these petite Tuxedo Cakes and clouds of white meringues, served with champagne. (For recipes, see pp. 108 & 122.) Top off the evening with Top Hat Shooters—just add two parts *Kahlua®* to shot glasses and very slowly pour in heavy cream.

Music: *Various Artists, "Pure Disco"; Various Artists, "Save the Last Dance [Soundtrack]"; Billie Holiday, "Jazz 'Round Midnight"*

Place Card: *Super Glue®* rhinestones to white tented place cards; spell out guests' initials for extra glitz. Napkins are nattily dressed in black bowties (for men) and rhinestone tiaras (for women). (Tiaras are available at most accessory stores.)

199

index

index

MUSIC

Free
Lifestyle web magazine subscription

Just visit
www.semi-homemade.com
today to subscribe!

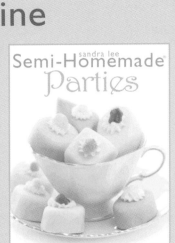

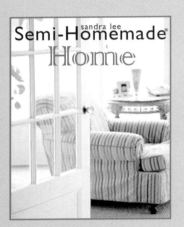

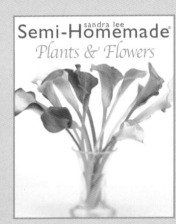

Each issue is filled with new, easy how-to projects, simple lifestyle tips, and an abundance of helpful hints. For busy people on a budget and on-the-go, the *Semi-Homemade® Magazine* is the perfect way to "have it all"…in the time you have.

tables & settings   fashion & beauty   home & garden   fabulous florals

perfect parties   entertaining & gatherings   gifts & giving

marvelous meals   music & movies   semi-homemaker's tips & tricks